How desolate my life would be,
How dark and dreary my nights and days,
If Jesus' face I did not see,
To brighten all earth's weary ways
I'm overshadowed by His mighty love
Love eternal, changeless pure.
Overshadowed by His mighty love
Rest is mine, serene, secure.
He died to ransom me from sin,
He lives to keep me day by day,
I'm overshadowed by his mighty love,
Love that brightens all my way.
With burdened heart I wandered long,
By grief and unbelief distressed;
But now I sing faith's happy song,
In Christ my Savior I am blest.
Now judgment fears no more alarm,
I dread no death, nor Satan's power;
The world for me has lost its charm,
God's grace sustains me every hour.

"Overshadowed"

A hymn by Harry A. Ironside

Overshadowed

By
Janeen Paczewitz

© 2008 Janeen Paczewitz
ISBN: 978-0-578-02037-2

Contents

Chapter   **Page**

Foreword..iii
Acknowledgements..v
1 Reflection..1
2 The Marshalls..5
3 A Loss..21
4 Some Distractions...33
5 Rage..43
6 Leila..59
7 Family Vacations..65
8 The Best Laid Plans…..79
9 Continuous Violations..93
10 Improvements and Relief.................................101
11 Transformation..115
12 Life After High School....................................119
13 Deadline..141
14 A New Life..159
15 Forgiveness...167
Epilogue..169

Foreword

Welcome to a journey not intended for the faint-hearted. Welcome to a true, heart-wrenching, soul stirring account of a young girl's worst nightmare, but also the great news that there is hope and healing from even the most evil of circumstances.

I have the humbling, awesome privilege of being Janeen's pastor's wife. I remember the first time Janeen ever came into the door of my Bible study – I was struck with the absolute glow of the Lord on her face, and a beautiful smile that I instinctively knew came from the inside. Over the next few weeks and months, I also came to anticipate her answers to questions, because I knew that she would give mature, Godly responses.

Janeen brought me a copy of this book and asked me to read it. I was so excited for her, and eagerly started on it that very evening. As I began to read the horrors that she went through, I have to be honest with you, I had to put the book down. Janeen's sweet, precious face kept flashing in my mind, and I just couldn't bear to think that she suffered this unthinkable abuse. But thanks be to God, I gathered up my strength and finished the book. I am so glad I did, because I saw Romans 8:28 lived out. "For we know that ALL things work together for the good of them that love the lord and are called according to His purpose."

I would strongly encourage you to put this book into the hands of those in your circle of influence who could not only grow from this book, but also to pass it on. Janeen is a happy, healthy, whole grandmother who has lived a fulfilling life. I watch her work with our young women, mentor them, and even rock babies! Her story is one of hope, healing, and most of all faith in a Heavenly Father who sustains and makes all things new.

Whatever the situation you find yourself in as you read this book, may God richly bless you. Janeen and I pray that this book will minister to you and bring healing.

- Angie Dennis

Angie Dennis is the wife of Jay Dennis, Senior Pastor of First Baptist Church at the Mall in Lakeland, Florida.

Acknowledgements

I give my deepest thanks to my family and friends for encouraging me to write my story, and to Sharon for her help. Thank you, Gil for your patience and words of wisdom while listening to my ideas. Thanks also to my son Chris for all your many hours of hard work in editing. I am proud and grateful.

Chapter 1

Reflection

In early September of 1989, my husband, Gil, my 12 year old son, Chris, and I had just finished moving into an apartment that was our temporary residence while we waited for construction on our new house to be completed. One morning while Gil was on his way to drop Chris off at school, I received a call from my stepmother, Rose. She was calling to tell me that my father who had been very sick was now in the hospital. I knew he wasn't doing well, but I prayed that he'd be able to hold on a little longer. I still needed a chance to get some things in order. I made sure Rose knew that my brother, Rick, and I would be on our way as soon as we could book a flight and pack our luggage. After that conversation, I immediately called Gil, then Rick, then a travel agent. I booked an evening flight that would arrive in Florida late that night. From the time I spoke with Rose, I couldn't stop thinking about my childhood.

Gil drove me to the airport, and reminded me that he and Chris would be praying for me. He knew how difficult this would be. Once Rick and I had stowed our carry-on bags in the overhead compartment and settled into our seats, our conversation gradually shifted from travel concerns to reminiscence about our childhood. We shared lots of stories during that flight. Some of them were common memories; some were secrets that had been kept until that night. Some were fond recollections, some were not.

Our plane landed in Ft. Lauderdale around 1:30 am. We were greeted by Reverend Daniels, who was the pastor of the church my parents attended. He was a kind and caring man with whom we had become acquainted during our previous trips to visit Rose and my dad. As he drove he told us that he had long talks with my dad, and was confident that he was ready to meet the Lord. We finally arrived at Memorial hospital in Hollywood at 2:00. Upon arriving at the hospital, Reverend Daniels explained that he had been there all day with my stepmother, and he needed to go home and get some rest. We told him we understood, and thanked him for all he had done.

Several questions started bouncing around in my head when we got out of the car. Would Dad be able to hear me? How would I know whether or not he can understand what I'm saying? Would this be the end of our relationship with Rose? Will she go to live with her sister? Time would tell. We made our way up to the floor my father was on. When the elevator doors opened, we stepped into the hall and started the seemingly endless walk toward the nurses' station. We were met by an intensive care nurse who correctly guessed who we were. She told us that she thought our dad was just hanging on until we arrived, and warned us to be careful of what we said because he was still very aware of everything going on around him.

My father's health had been deteriorating as a result of a lifelong battle with diabetes. He had been in the hospital for nearly a week following a sudden loss of strength and weight. His doctor had attempted to take a bone marrow sample from his sternum, but during the procedure my father went into shock and was not expected to recover. He was now on a ventilator, barely able to move or communicate in any way. A couple of days earlier when Rose called to deliver the news of Dad's condition, she begged me to forgive her for allowing him to be placed on life support. They had agreed that she would sign a Do Not Resuscitate form, but in the confusion of his rapid decline she had forgotten to do so. I assured her that I was anything but angry with her. In fact, I was certain that it was God's sovereign plan that my dad be kept alive until Rick and I spoke with him one last time.

As the nurse walked with us to dad's room, she told us that Rose had not left his side since he came into the intensive care unit almost three days earlier. She suggested that we try to convince Rose to go home and get some sleep rather than spend another night on the recliner the hospital staff had brought in for her. With the bright lights and regular visits from doctors and nurses, it was unlikely that she had gotten much rest. The nurse added that if we had any last words for dad, we would need to speak up soon. With that she took us into the large room that was separated from the hallway by a glass wall. The draperies had been pulled partially closed to provide a modicum of privacy. On the far wall was a very large window. I remember looking out into the night and wondering how long it would be before my father would be on his way beyond the darkness to meet God. The nurse gently touched Rose to let her know we had arrived. Startled, she sat up, pulled the blanket off herself, and began to cry all at the same time. Rick and I hugged her and told her that we were there for her. Through her tears she again asked us to forgive her for allowing Dad to be put on a ventilator. We told her once more that we weren't upset with her, and tried to ease her feelings of guilt. She told us about the time she had spent in the hospital, and the discussions she had with Dad before the recent turn of events. She told us how much she loved him and us. It was a very sweet few minutes.

Then it was time for us to speak with Dad. Rick walked around to the right side of the bed and Rose and I stayed on the left side. Rose gently put her right arm under his neck and began to rub his left arm. She softly announced, "Stephen, dear; the children are here." Dad blinked his eyes. Rose moved away to let me come as close to him as I could. The diabetes had made him a virtual prisoner in his own body. He was blind and had no feeling in his hands or feet. He was swollen and his organs were shutting down. He knew that he was dying. As I looked at what had become of this man who had once been very strong, memories of my childhood flooded my mind. I felt overwhelming compassion because of the suffering he was enduring as well as the uncertainty of the judgment he would soon face.

Chapter 2

The Marshalls

Some of my first memories are of an aging neighborhood in southwest Detroit. The demographic of our part of the city could be described as a sort of alphabet soup – everything from A to Z. Many people were immigrants and almost everyone was poorly educated. There were Hungarians, Russians, and Germans; Catholics, Lutherans, and Anglicans. My grandparents, Stephen and Ada, were immigrants from England. My grandfather and his brother had decided to bring their families to the United States when my father (also named Stephen) was about 18 months old. Life in America was not what my grandmother thought it would be. Grandpa began frequenting the local bar and became a drunk, often buying a round for all of his "friends". Grandma eventually decided she'd had enough. She took young Stephen back to England for a visit and stayed there for almost nine years. Grandpa gave up drinking, went to England, and convinced his wife to return to the United States with him. Grandma never saw England again, but Grandpa quickly resumed his trips to the bar.

My father had a difficult time adjusting to life with additional discipline. Returning to Detroit meant that he now had to obey his Mother, Father, and his Aunt Emma who lived across the street. Dorothy and Winifred, his tattletale cousins, added to his trouble. My dad occasionally told us of his attempt to please his father by pushing his car into the alley to wash it. His good intentions only resulted in discipline when Aunt Emma claimed that he had driven the car without permission. At times he purposely misbehaved, knowing that either his cousins or their mother were watching and would report to his father. Despite his rebellious nature, my father was a decent student. But as many boys did, he dropped out of school in the tenth grade to begin working.

My mother, Verna, was born out of wedlock. Her parents, Miriam and George, planned to marry as soon as my grandfather returned from World War I, but he was killed before he even received the news that he was going to be a father. As it was socially unacceptable in 1913 to have an illegitimate child, most women in my grandmother's situation would have given their baby up for adoption. Miriam, however, was determined to keep her baby. With very little education and insufficient income, that proved to be a very difficult task. She tried working as a maid, but was unable to manage working and caring for a child at the same time. Verna's health began to decline as a result. Realizing that she needed help, Miriam wrote a letter to her mother (my great grandmother). For about a year, my mother stayed with my great aunt and great grandmother who nursed her back to health. When Miriam received a photograph of her healthy, happy daughter, she decided she wanted her back. She made the trip to Wisconsin to reunite with Verna, and soon made her way to Montreal. Around the time my mom was eight years old, Miriam married a man she had not known long. He married her on the condition that she would not burden him with the responsibility of caring for a child. The solution was for Verna to spend most of her childhood living in boarding homes. As my grandparents moved from state to state, my mother moved from boarding house to boarding house. Fortunately her mother and stepfather had the decency to keep her close enough for occasional visits.

Verna managed to be fairly successful in school despite the hardships she endured. She bought her own schoolbooks with the money she earned by working at the boarding house. At ten years old, she contracted scarlet fever and was taken to the hospital. To keep the disease from spreading, all of her books and the one doll she owned were incinerated. Once she had recovered, she began working full time as a maid instead of returning to school. At the age of fourteen, she learned that her mother was very ill. She arrived at the door to Miriam's hospital room only too see that it was too late - her mother had just died. Years later, during the Great Depression, she met my father at the church where she played guitar and led singing in her youth group. After just six months they were married, even though my father was unemployed and had no savings. She was 21, and he was 23. Because they were basically penniless, they moved in with Grandpa and Grandma Marshall. Dad's parents welcomed them into their home.

My grandfather was a hard worker and managed to stay employed during the Great Depression. He held a full time job at the Solvay Processing Company, and his spare time was spent building wheel barrels, cabinets and lawn chairs. He earned enough income to own three houses on our street and provide for his son and daughter-in-law. My grandmother was a kind woman who was loved by everyone. She waited on her husband hand and foot except for the times he would make demands while lying in bed drunk. I can still hear him calling out in his English accent, "Ada! Oh, Ada! I say Ada! Hark you! Do ye hear me? Fetch me my cigarette!"

Sometimes my grandmother would fire back, "Dash you! Get them yourself!" She knew he was drunk, and didn't want him smoking in bed.

While he was quite unpleasant when he had been drinking, he was a lot of fun when he was sober. They were far from perfect, but my mother developed a strong relationship with her in-laws and loved them very much. A new addition to the family came in 1936 when my older brother, David, was born. I came along just eleven months later. We were often mistaken for twins. For a while I was known as my parents' lucky charm because my dad found a job soon after I was born. For the first time in her life, my Mom had a home and a family.

This home was the first of two houses we lived in as I was growing up. Six of us crammed ourselves into that old gray house on Dragoon Street: Grandpa, Grandma, Mom,

Dad, and my brother, David, and me. Several details of its features stand out in my memory. There were the two tiny bedrooms we slept in – one for Grandma and Grandpa, and one for Mom, Dad, David and me. After David and I were put to bed, it was time for my parents' duet. Mom had bought a guitar on layaway, paying 25 cents a week until it was hers. Dad played a second-hand accordion that worked well enough for him. They didn't begin playing until they thought we were already asleep, but I was often lulled by the sound of their music. In the sitting room at the front of the house was a davenport from England, a very large armchair, and a rocking chair over which David and I often fought. The dining room was home to a potbelly stove and a very large, old dining table. Several chairs surrounded it, but my favorite spot was on a long bench made of wood and leather that sat against the wall. From there I could see a picture of my dad as a child, dressed in a sailor suit and sitting at that very table. Looking at the picture made me happy. I loved my dad and the stories he would tell us.

In the kitchen was a wood-burning stove on which Grandma and Mom did all the cooking. I remember the sink with its large drain board and long neck faucet where Grandpa would scrub his false teeth. As a little girl I tried unsuccessfully to take mine out as well. There was also a white cupboard with glass doors built into the wall. Inside were all of my grandparents' dishes from England. My grandmother reserved one dish for David and me. She kept the dish filled with candy canes she had carefully broken into small pieces. When we were well behaved, Grandma would bring down the candy dish for us. It was a special treat, since my dad's job didn't pay enough to buy much candy for us. That was one of the ways Grandma showed her skill in stretching money. After she passed away, my parents found money tucked away in hiding places all over the house. Grandpa held onto his paycheck and only gave grandma money after drinking with the boys down at Victor's Bar at the end of our street.

Grandpa Marshall was Anglican, and Grandma was Catholic, but none of us attended church regularly until I was seven years old. Even so, my parents often taught my brothers and me about God. They told us about Jesus, and that he had died on a cross to atone for our sin. Praying was also a very big part of our lives. We always prayed at mealtime and before going to bed. At the age of five, I knelt at the couch in our living room with mom and dad beside me and asked Jesus to forgive me of my sin and help me to live for Him.

We lived just one block from Fort Wayne. The fort, which was situated on the banks of the Detroit River, was the main storage facility for the vehicles and weapons manufactured in Detroit during World Wars I and II. Early each morning we would hear the bugler play his wake up call, followed in the evening by the mournful sound of "Taps". One block to the north there were five sets of railroad tracks that intersected our street. Passenger, commercial, and military trains frequently passed through the neighborhood.

Much of this increased traffic was a direct result of World War II. As the war progressed, the need for men, machines, and weapons increased. Companies that wanted to move in to our neighborhood to build factories and scrap yards bought many nearby houses. While the spread of heavy industry made our neighborhood less attractive, it did bring many jobs to the area. People without much education and those who had recently immigrated could earn more money and had a chance at upward mobility.

While the war brought opportunity for some, we all faced daily reminders of our vulnerability. While at school, air raid drills would send us to the shelters marked by ominous orange and black Civil Defense signs. If the sirens were started at night, our windows would have to be covered with room darkening shades to keep light from escaping through the windows. This would make targets less visible to enemy bombers above. Civil Defense officials patrolled the streets to make sure that everyone followed instructions. The first instance of noncompliance would result in a warning; the second would bring a fine. Government rationing of gasoline and various food items meant that we had to use stamps and tokens to buy many of our daily necessities. We were allowed to purchase a limited amount of sugar, butter, cheese, and meat.

My parents put us to bed at 7:30 every night, earlier than the other children in our neighborhood. They made an exception on the night of August 14, 1945. It was a calm and beautiful summer evening that suddenly came alive with the sound of car horns, church bells, and people shouting in the street. Puzzled by the commotion, my parents hurried out of the house to be greeted by ecstatic neighbors celebrating the end of World War II. They came back to get us out of bed and dressed us so we wouldn't miss what proved to be one of the most memorable days in our nation's history.

****

The other house my grandfather owned was next to the one we had been living in. He had been keeping it as a rental property, but eventually his tenants moved out and he decided that he would like us to move into it. His offer was an incredible blessing. This house was slightly larger than the other, and it had three bedrooms instead of two. It was basically rectangular, with the bedrooms sitting end-to-end along the right side, and the common areas on the left. At the front was the sitting room. Behind it was the living room, then the dining room. The kitchen was at the back of the house, with our only bathroom next to it on the right.

I could hardly wait to have my own bedroom, and now I was about to have a big one (or at least one that looked big to me). In my room I had a large metal bed. At night I would tap the headboard with my fingernails to create a percussive melody. Many nights I was scolded by my mom or dad, "Janeen! Will you stop playing with that bed and go to sleep right now?!" In my closet I had a cardboard box where I kept my toys. I had a recurring dream that I went into the closet, and moved the box to one side revealing a door on the back wall. I'd open that door, walk down a hallway to another door, only to find another hallway with a door at the end. I had the same dream over and over again for several years.

In front of the house there was a porch where we would sit in wooden chairs my grandfather had made. The first room you would enter through the front door was a small coatroom. On the other side of the coatroom's back wall was the first bedroom. To the left was an archway that led to the living room, which held all the usual furniture: a sofa with a matching chair, a bookcase, and a small table.

The next room was the sitting room. In one corner of the room was a daybed that eventually served as my bed after my grandfather moved in with us. Next to it was the dining chair my grandfather always sat in while he watched wrestling matches with my father. My parents' bedroom was to the right of the sitting room. It was just large enough for a double bed, a dresser, and a nightstand. It had a tiny closet that had a drape instead of a door.

Walking further into the house, you would enter the dining room. We had a large oak table where we only ate dinner on special occasions. It was reserved for holidays or visits from our pastor or missionaries who had made an appearance at our church. Somewhat ironically, we also used it as a makeshift ping-pong table, and for playing board games. A window on the left wall had lace curtains that hung in front of green room-darkening shades. On the opposite wall was a large buffet that was adorned by a pair of beautiful vases. The vases, which had been brought from England, were a wedding gift to my grandparents. Next to the buffet sat a very old radio. Four legs raised it about a foot off the floor, and it had doors on the front that hid the controls. Fabric that was stretched behind a dark wooden lattice covered the speakers. Grandpa would listen to boxing matches, and my brothers and I listened to the Lone Ranger. We only got to do this when my parents weren't home. They felt that either one was too violent for children, so my Grandfather made a deal with us…he would let us listen to the Lone Ranger as long as we didn't tell our parents that he listened to boxing. Sometimes he would break another rule and leave us at home alone to buy hamburgers at White Castle on Fort Street, not far from our house.

Beyond the dining room was our kitchen, which housed all the obvious items. At the back wall was a sink with a drain board at each end, and drawers that held our silverware, dishcloths, and cooking utensils. The window over the sink allowed a view of the backyard. Looking through it we could see the roof over the exterior door to our basement, and just beyond it, the sour cherry tree from which my mother made many pies. Along the same wall stood an old gas stove which had an empty space next to it until my grandfather bought us a Scottish terrier. Then the spot became the designated area for our dog's bed. In the center of the room we had a maple table with six chairs that Grandpa refinished for us many times. It seemed to be the thing he loved to do most. On the right wall was another window from which we could once again see my grandparents' house. On the opposite side of the room was a pantry where we kept most of our food.

Sometimes I would sneak into it and steal a piece of bread to relieve the pangs of hunger that kept me awake at night. Aside from its normal use, the kitchen also served as a temporary roller skating rink after my grandfather bought skates for David and me. The floor was scheduled to be replaced a week later, so it was the perfect place to learn. Our one and only bathroom was at the left end of the kitchen. It was quite large for the size of the house, and it had a window high on one wall. In fact, it was too high for me to pull the curtains closed for privacy. I hated that window.

There was another porch on the right side of the house outside the kitchen. It had windows on the outside wall, and a door on the front and back. From the porch we could look out and see my grandparents' house and yard. In the winter it kept some of the cold air from coming into the kitchen, and provided a place for us to take off our boots so we wouldn't track snow across the floor. It also served as the home for our icebox. One benefit of those cold winter months was the fact that we didn't have to buy much ice to keep our food refrigerated.

Some of my fondest memories of living in that house are from the holidays. Our Christmas traditions began on Christmas Eve with my parents reading the story of Christ's birth. Then we would say our prayers and would be sent to bed with the assurance that if we went right to sleep, Santa would visit our house. We were each given one very long winter stocking to hang on the doorknob of our room for Santa to fill. Like all children, I was so excited that falling asleep was next to impossible. That was how I found out who was actually filling my stocking each year. One Christmas Eve as I lay awake in bed, I heard our stockings being taken from the door to be filled with fruit, nuts, candy and a toy or two. To my surprise, the voices I also heard were the familiar whispers of my parents. It wasn't too disappointing to learn who was really delivering the surprises as long as they kept coming each year.

As soon as we woke on Christmas morning, we would jump out of bed and hurry to our bedroom doors to find our stockings filled to the top. Toys were always on top, then an assortment of nuts, a large apple and orange, and a candy cane hidden somewhere inside. After we emptied the stockings, it was time to gather around the tree where mom and dad would hand out our gifts. Grandma knew that our father didn't have enough money to buy much, so she always made sure we had a great Christmas. Once our gifts were unwrapped, my mother and grandmother would prepare a large breakfast. It usually consisted of raisin bread toast, bacon, eggs, and slices of oranges and apples. If my father wasn't working (he worked every other Christmas day) we would skip lunch and have an early dinner around two o'clock instead of four o'clock. Sitting still at the dinner table on Christmas was always a challenge for my brothers and me. All we wanted to do was get back to playing with our toys.

Halloween was a fun time at our house as well. We weren't allowed to trick-or-treat in the neighborhood when we were very young, but Grandma managed to make it fun for us. Each doorway in the house was a different station where we were given pieces of fruit or a candy cane. Once we were old enough to go trick-or-treating on our own, there was one spot that was off limits. Each year, the bags of potato chips given out at Victor's Bar were a temptation. All our friends went there, and we always wanted to join them. We eventually gave in, hoping that if we ate the chips before we got home our parents would never find out. The problem with our plan was that we forgot that Grandpa was a frequent customer at the bar. A few of the men that were there recognized us, and mentioned to our grandfather that they had seen us.

Things began to change a bit when I was five and a half. My baby brother Rick was born, and while mom was in the hospital it was up to me to make up for her absence. My grandmother was in poor health, so she wasn't able to provide much help. One job that Dad assigned to me was scrubbing the kitchen floor on my hands and knees. That floor looked so very big to me at that age. I thought I'd never finish. The floor seemed to grow larger and larger as I scrubbed under the radiator and table. My knees hurt, my back hurt, and I just wanted it to be done. As dad checked to see if I had done a good job, he found that I hadn't reached all the way under the table and under the radiator, so I was sent back to do the job all over again. Upon his next inspection he found that there was too much water on the floor, so I had to start over a third time. It didn't matter that at only five years old my hands weren't strong enough to wring all the water out of the cloth. I couldn't wait until my mom was back on her feet. She came home in an ambulance and had to stay in bed for two weeks. Filling in for her meant that I had to do some growing up in a hurry.

With a new baby in the house, I always wanted to take care of him until one of my friends came over to play. Unfortunately, he became a responsibility that I couldn't so easily escape. Before playing, I had to take him for a long walk. My mother would put him in his buggy, and off we would go – up and down the street until he fell asleep or mom called for us to come home. Once he outgrew the buggy, I took him for rides in our little red wagon. My mother also showed me how to iron clothes, dust the house, and (of course) wash the dishes. Since I was so young, I had to kneel on a chair to reach the ironing board or the sink. My role as mother's little helper eventually left me with no friends and a weakened relationship with my brother. David and I had been best friends, but taking care of Rick afforded little time to play and have fun with him like I used to.

Starting school was a big deal for me, as it is for most children. I was in the morning kindergarten class, but liked it so much that I convinced my mother that I was supposed to be in the afternoon class as well. As the roll was being taken that afternoon, the teacher called out my name. This time it wasn't to make sure I was there – it was because I wasn't supposed to be there. It was a long, difficult trek to her desk. I'd been found out before class had even started. Instead of sending me home, I was allowed to sit in the corner until school was over. Watching from a distance and not being allowed to participate was no fun, so I ended up wishing I were at home playing anyway. I also knew that I would have to tell my mom that I lied, so I didn't try that again. I enjoyed school until the day I missed the opportunity to use the restroom. My class had already gone as a group, so when I raised my hand and asked if I could be excused I received punishment instead. My teacher sent me to the coatroom for the rest of the day, and was not allowed to watch a movie with my classmates. They had lots of laughs about the puddle flowing from under the door while I sat inside, wet with urine and tears. It was a very long time before I looked forward to school again.

Illness was a regular part of my childhood, and I missed classes often. I was plagued with chicken pox, measles, tonsillitis, colds, earaches, scarlet fever, and numerous stomach problems. David was generally in good health, so he was able to be in school most of the time. His grades were much better than mine as a result. I had to struggle so hard to keep up that school became drudgery for me. Some days I would beg to stay at home with my little brother. That request was never granted.

When I was seven years old, David and I started attending Sunday school at a church down the street from our house. We enjoyed it, so we decided to stay for the morning sermon. While we were standing with the rest of the congregation to sing, a man came to us and asked us to come 'to the back of the church. He told us that we couldn't stay because our parents weren't with us. Feeling rejected and disappointed made our walk home seem to take twice as long as usual. Little did we know that this would end up as a blessing in disguise.

    My father couldn't afford to buy a car, but he was trying to save for one. He had taken up photography with the intent to use his pictures as reference for oil paintings. He hoped that with enough practice his art would be good enough to sell. My dad abandoned that plan when we told him what had happened at church. That was the last straw. Dad sold all his photography equipment and all of his instruments. They provided just enough money to pay for a very old Dodge. It was so old that it had shades with tassels on them in all the back windows. We were glad they were there because we loved pulling them down and we didn't want our friends to see us in that old tank. It may have been ugly, but for about three years it transported all of us to church as a family. When it finally broke down beyond repair, it was back to the bus stops for us. Our trips to and from church required us to take two busses each way. Waiting for a bus in the winter wind was a less than comfortable experience. The snow always seemed to fall on Saturday, so we would have to pull on our boots and trudge through the deep white powder. Occasionally we would run from one stop to another hoping that the driver would see us and wait. Sometimes it worked, sometimes it didn't. Several years passed before we were able to get another car.

Chapter 3

A Loss

Grandpa was still drinking heavily, and it was becoming a major problem. On several occasions the police came to our house in the middle of the night to tell us that they had taken him to jail for sitting on the railroad tracks. After a night of drinking he often became depressed to the point of being suicidal. The officers sympathized with my family and released Grandpa, but assured us that they wouldn't continue to be as lenient. The feeling of security I had in that small house was beginning to slip away. Because visiting Victor's Bar was the only social activity in which my grandfather participated, he was beside himself when my father forbade him from going back. David and I knew what he was lacking, and in our simplistic way we would tell him that he needed to trust Jesus.

One night he gave in to our pleas and came to church with the rest of the family. To everyone's surprise, he listened intently to the sermon and it touched him deeply. He gave his life to God, and was changed instantly. He had been a drunk for decades, but from that day on he never touched another drop of alcohol. God even gave him the strength to resist temptation when his old friends would beg him to come back to Victor's Bar with them. Grandma received the greatest blessing from her husband's transformation. She saw him become the man she always hoped he would be, and she felt that her life was complete.

My grandfather made his life changing decision just in time. About three months after his conversion, my grandmother contracted pneumonia. I don't remember how exactly how long she was sick, but it wasn't more than a few days. My parents told us that she needed lots of rest, and instructed us to not disturb her. No matter how badly we wanted to go into her room and be with her, we didn't go any further than the doorway where we stood looking in at her. The window shade was drawn, but there was enough light for us to see her face. Her eyes were always closed. Mom and Dad finally called us to come into Grandma's room, but it was only to say goodbye. The doctor was on his way to the house to see her, and we assumed she was going to the hospital. As we stood at her bedside, her eyes remained closed and she lay still the whole time. I don't think she even knew we were there. My parents told us that she was going to stay asleep and would go to heaven to be with Jesus. We stayed there for a few minutes, then my mom and dad took us out of the room. We had school that day, and no exception was made. When we came back home, we found out that grandma had been taken away and wouldn't be coming back.

The funeral was held a few days later. My brothers and I were dressed in our Sunday best, and we walked the same route we took to buy our groceries. I remember standing outside the store looking across the street at the funeral home. I wanted to go in and see grandma, but at the same time I was afraid. We all held hands as we walked into the room where she was laid out. I could smell the beautiful flowers that decorated the room. Only a few more steps and I would be in front of the casket. Finally she was in sight. There she was, lying so still and very beautiful. Mom and dad had purchased a very pretty navy blue dress with a white lace collar. The buttons on it fascinated me, and I will always remember them. They were arranged in four pairs, with Chinese brad loops that curled around them. Her hands grasped Lilies of the Valley, her favorite flower. She grew them in her backyard, and brought some into the house as often as she could. It was their scent that I had smelled when I walked into the room. I wasn't afraid anymore…just very sad, and very lonely.

Grandpa didn't do well without his beloved Ada. Mom took on new responsibilities to help him. She cleaned his house and she made his lunch before work each day. He joined us for breakfast every morning, and for dinner every evening. Even with our attempts to provide comfort, grief made it very difficult for him to continue working and before long he retired. My parents decided that he should come to live with us. The only drawback was that this meant someone had to give up his or her bedroom, and I was the one chosen to make the sacrifice. Baby Rick was moved into David's room, and the sitting room became my bedroom. This didn't mean that the room was remodeled or even that the furniture was moved. It simply meant that I would now be sleeping on the daybed. Unfortunately, my parents didn't want the cushions placed on the floor; I wasn't allowed to unfold it. The couch was where I slept, and the floor was where I often woke up until David moved out fifteen years later.

My grandfather wasn't the only one who was hurting. I cried myself to sleep every night for months. Each one of us was devastated by her sudden absence. David and I lost our tenderhearted matriarch. Grandpa lost his source of strength. My mother lost her best friend, and my father lost his conscience.

My dad's initial deviations from normal parenting and discipline seem mild in comparison with the abuse to which we eventually became accustomed. I remember one of the first times he let his temper get the best of him. At bath time one evening, Dad came to the three of us, looked at me, and said "You first." He heated up the water tank, filled the tub, and told me to undress and get in. At seven years old, I was mature enough to want some privacy so I told him I could give myself a bath. That was my first mistake. I was completely submerged in nearly scalding water before I even had a chance to realize that my clothes had been pulled off. Handfuls of soapsuds were pushed through my hair and onto my face without a chance for me to take a breath. When I tried to inhale, I sucked the suds into my nose and began to cry. I had pressed Dad's buttons again…he couldn't stand a sissy. He threw cold water in my face, and then told me to blow my nose. He got a bit of a surprise when blood came pouring out, and fortunately it was enough to make him calm down. I thought Dad was just having a bad day. He had a new baby and a sick wife, and he just wasn't used to all the responsibility of working full time and taking care of the household.

Not long after this, Dad started making remarks about how I was "developing". He'd often pull up my blouse to have a look, and then amuse himself with insulting comment that prompted his own ugly laughter. Sometimes he would ask me embarrassing questions, and if I didn't respond, he would grab me by the hair and shout, "I was talking to you, and you will give me an answer before I shake it out of you!" If my answer wasn't satisfactory, he would start shaking me until I thought my head would fall off. Once he turned me loose I often fell to the floor, which made me vulnerable to another attack. Occasionally he would keep me from standing by pushing my chest against the floor with his foot on my back. I was his prisoner until he was finished with my "punishment", which was usually some method of forced contortion that stretched my joints to their limits. Sometimes he would pull my foot up to touch the back of my head. Other times he chose to hyperextend my thumb toward my forearm. He also liked to twist my arm behind my back, or grab my wrist and rotate my outstretched limb beyond its normal range of motion. The way he treated us was dependent upon his mood each day, but the abuse was not always a product of anger. It was more of a hobby that occasionally found purpose in his anger. An assault could be triggered by walking past him, or by simply being in the same room.

At first I kept trying to make excuses for him. Maybe his work day didn't go well. Grandpa probably made him mad. He didn't get much sleep because the baby kept him awake. As much as I tried to make sense of his behavior, none of the explanations I imagined could justify the terrible things he was doing to us. If his standards weren't met when we did our chores, Punishment came swiftly and fiercely. Spankings quickly turned into full-fledged beatings that left us with large welts on our arms, legs, and buttocks. We had to wear long sleeves in the summer so the evidence would be hidden from our friends and their parents. During one assault, Dad was spanking my brother with a wooden yardstick that was almost a half-inch thick and had a metal cap at each end. David was made to bend over the front edge of a dining room chair with his head pointing toward the back of the chair. After a few blows he slid backward, lowering his backside toward his heels to avoid being struck again. With the next swing, my father brought the stick down on his back with such force that David arched his back in pain then lunged forward again, smashing his lower lip against the edge of the chair. My mother shouted, "Stephen, stop! His lip is bleeding!" Concerned only with dishing out a proper punishment, my father's response was, "Good for him! He's still going to get what I promised him!" After a few more lashes my dad finally stopped, and David made his escape.

My mom chased after him to see if he was alright, and found out that he wasn't. When David hit the chair, his teeth had pierced through his lower lip leaving an incision about a quarter of an inch long.

Even the simplest of daily tasks revolved around trying to protect myself from my father. Since I no longer had a bedroom of my own, I hung my clothes in my brothers' bedroom or put them in my dresser that was kept in the bathroom. If I needed to change my clothes, that was done behind a chair in the dining room or in the bathroom if it was unoccupied. With five other people in the house, changing in the bathroom was a rare luxury. I eventually learned how to put on a new set of clothes under the ones I was already wearing, and I became a quick change artist. Sometimes I was allowed to use my mom and dad's bedroom to change, but I had to make sure that dad was nowhere around. He would come in and sit on the bed to watch me, telling me to go ahead with what I was doing. If he saw that I was changing with my clothes still on, he would come around the table before I could get away or finish dressing, and pull the garment in progress off of me. It didn't matter to him whether it was my underwear, bra, slip, or a dress. His hands were all over me. I would try to break free, but he'd grab my arm and twist it behind my back so I couldn't move. While I cried out in pain he would grab whichever part of my body he felt like groping, and when he was finished, push me away with the words "You big crybaby! Get out of my sight!" With my bed being in the middle of the house, it was very convenient for my dad to stop by whenever he pleased. Since I was no match for his strength, I would lay face-down with my arms beneath me. When he came to my bed I pretended to be asleep, or when I was older I tried to convince him that it was my time of the month. Sometimes I would lie facing the wall so I could bring my knees up to my chest and curl into a fetal position. That didn't work because the couch was so small that I would fall off. Dad would grab me by the hair, pull me up, and throw me back onto the couch and pounce on me. He stifled my cries for my mother by burying my face under a pillow. I often thought and even wished he would suffocate me. I tried to so hard to fight him off, but at 175 pounds, he weighed nearly three times as much as me. From the moment he finished until the moment I fell asleep, I would lie in bed crying and begging God to let me die. In the morning as I got ready for school, my mom would sometimes see that my eyes were swollen from crying. She would ask me if I felt alright, and I always told her that I was. I knew that there was nothing that she would or could do about it.

After school, I was always on the lookout for him. He came home from work at about four thirty each day. While helping my mother prepare dinner, I would stand at the kitchen window so I would know when he arrived. I'd drop whatever I was doing and head for the bathroom just to keep him from fondling me. If it was occupied, the fight would begin as soon as my father came into the house and set his lunchbox down. Mom tried to intervene, but my father would just bark, "Stay out of this! It's none of your business!" Rick taught me that if I let my body go limp I could slip out of my dad's grasp. That just made him angry, but I did it anyway. I saw no reason to make it easy for him to get what he wanted.

All I could do was plead with God, "Where are you?! Help me!"

I began to hate my father, and I went to bed every night wishing that my grandmother was still alive. I knew she wouldn't let him be so cruel to us. At the same time, I knew God was aware of everything that was happening, but I couldn't understand why he would let it continue. If David and I were caught whispering we would get in trouble, so we took long walks and vented to each other about the hell our lives were becoming. I could see from the beginning that my brother was unable to cope with the abuse. His only source of hope seemed to be the thought that one day he would find a way to get revenge.

My brother and I reacted very differently when mistreated. I would become quiet and withdrawn, while David sought revenge. He didn't dare to retaliate against my father, but he often evened the score with other children. Sometimes he would steal from the "guilty" party and either give the item away or simply destroy it. He also had a trick he liked to play on people. Roger was one neighbor with whom he never got along, which made him the perfect target. David had an idea for a prank, and used the layout of our property to his advantage. Houses in our neighborhood were so close together, that there was no room for a driveway. Our garage stood at the back of the yard, directly behind our house. The main doors were on the far side, and opened up to an alley that ran behind all the houses on our street. David chose a spot in the back yard just a few feet in front of the left corner of the garage and dug a hole about ten inches deep and 8 inches wide. He filled it with water, covered it with paper, and then hid the paper by carefully sprinkling a layer of dirt over it. When he finished, he invited Roger over to play. Roger entered the yard from the alley, and traipsed along the left side of the garage. Not more than two steps after he rounded the corner, he stomped down into the muddy pit as planned. I suppose it wasn't until then that David realized that he had also dug a hole for himself. Roger immediately raced home to tell his mother, who in turn told my parents. David was punished accordingly, and was made to repair the damage to the lawn. He was also relegated to playing in the backyard without any friends. He never seemed to learn his lesson, though. He always seemed to prefer the temporary satisfaction of payback.

Another of David's ill-conceived plans came to fruition one day when Mom was busy cleaning house. He called me outside to show me that he could make me "spin like a top". He grabbed me and coiled a rope around my arms so quickly and tightly that I didn't have time to escape. My terrified protests fell on deaf ears. Once he had me wrapped up, he pulled on the free end of the rope as hard as he could. I only completed about half a rotation before I lost my balance and fell forward. Having my arms restrained stopped me from breaking my fall, and I wasn't even lucky enough to simply land on the ground. On my way down, the bottom edges of my two front teeth slammed into the steel cap of a pipe that protruded about three feet from the ground. The pain in my mouth was excruciating. David screamed as he frantically tried to free me from the rope. He helped me to my feet and ran up the porch steps and shouted for Mom. Finally hearing him over the noise of the vacuum, she raced over to him and tried to understand what had happened. In his state of panic, David had completely lost the ability to communicate. Mom attempted to snap him out of it with a smack across the face, but by that time I had staggered into her line of sight. She glanced beyond David to see another hysterical child, this one with the added excitement of a face that was bleeding profusely. Blood poured from my nose, mouth, and chin, and was now covering my hands and streaming down my forearms. As my mother guided me into the house, I described what had happened to the best of my ability. We went into the bathroom, where she retrieved a clean washcloth and dampened with cool water from the sink. Afraid to hear her answer, I asked if I had lost my front teeth. "No…" she said, "I think they are in there." She tilted my head back and looked at the bottom edge of my swollen gums. Sure enough, there were my teeth, shoved all the way up to where their roots were supposed to anchor them. They had been buried so deep that she could hardly see them.

After cleaning me up a bit, she brought out another damp cloth. With the knuckle of her index finger behind my gums and her thumb in front, she gently squeezed and pulled each tooth down to where it was supposed to be. I couldn't believe the relief I felt. With a swollen face, split lips, and a lacerated chin my mother rushed me to the dentist's office. The dentist told my mother that she had done the right thing, and there was nothing more he could do at that time. About two weeks later I woke up with pain behind my upper lip and a very swollen face. With another trip to the dentist we found out that my tooth was dying and had created an abscess. My parents only had enough money to treat the abscess, so the tooth stayed where it was and eventually turned black with decay.

While I believe the violent consequences of David's actions were unintentional, it seems clear to me that his physically domineering behavior was a trait he had learned from our father.

Chapter 4

Some Distractions

Fortunately, there were some improvements and distractions that made life more bearable. It was such a thrill to finally get a telephone in our house. They only came in one color: black. We also had to work around the fact that it was operating on a party line, which meant that we shared the line with several of our neighbors. If we were using the phone and one of the neighbors wanted to make a call, they had to pick up the handset and ask to use the phone or simply had to wait until we hung up. Some people would get annoyed and stay on the line longer just to irritate their neighbor. That was enough to start a cycle of phone rage. The person waiting to make a call would then eavesdrop on their neighbor's conversation. Sometimes this was enough to make the current user hang up, but often they'd just pick up the handset again and return the favor of eavesdropping. At times, my brother and I listened in on our neighbor's conversations for fun, but if Grandpa saw us he would say, "You know…listeners hear no good of themselves." That was usually enough to make us hang up. The most important thing about having a phone was that we could call my mother's cousin, Edna, who lived in Wisconsin. They had kept in touch over the years, but only by mail.

When I was thirteen, my parents decided it was time to do something about the constant sore throats that Rick and I suffered from. They took us to the doctor, who recommended a tonsillectomy for each of us. It was quite a while before the procedure could be done, because if I wasn't sick, my brother was. Neither one of us looked forward to the operation. We knew our throats were going to be very sore, but I kept thinking that maybe this could be my way out of the life I hated so deeply. I was drawn to the idea that if I could hold my breath while sinking into the effects of the anesthesia, maybe I would stop breathing for ever.

The day came, and Rick and I were as scared as we could be. We spent the morning answering questions and undergoing a routine exam. After that, the nurses delivered the bad news that we were ready. We were given a shot and taken to the operating room. My last thought as I lay on the table was to hold my breath so I could die.

The next thing I remember is the sound of my mother's voice comforting me as I began to wake. Once I was alert, she asked how I was feeling (other than my predictably sore throat). She told me that the nurse had to call my doctor to my room because I had stopped breathing after the operation. It hadn't happened quite the way I planned, but the result would have been the same had the nurse not been paying such close attention. I made no mention of my disappointment. My mother had enough pain in her life, and that would have only hurt her more.

Rick and I healed quickly and were back to school in no time. As time progressed, we realized that the recurring sore throats had stopped. The only downside was that I missed fewer days of school. Even that was a blessing since I needed all the help I could get with my grades.

The school year eventually ended, and summer vacation was upon us. There was a minister named Malachi Cook who attended our church. His poor health kept him from working full time, but he occasionally filled in for our pastor. Reverend Cook and his wife loved children, though they never had any of their own. They helped pay the cost for a few children to go to camp each year. One year they were kind enough to help my family.

The children went to camp in two groups: first the boys, then the girls. David paved the way for me, and I knew he would be writing letters to tell me all about the fun he was having. I waited anxiously to hear from him. After he had been gone a couple of days, the mailman came and I ran out to meet him. Sure enough there were three envelopes from David. One for me, and one for each of my parents. I tore mine open but as I began to read, my heart sank. I couldn't believe what I was reading! What is there to hate about summer camp? How could he possibly want to come home? He had written that the only thing he did enjoy was learning to row a boat. With that news, I wasn't sure whether or not I was ready for camp. There was no getting out of it anyway. I couldn't let Reverend Cook down...he had already paid for my trip. On top of that, mom had borrowed money from grandpa to buy Rick and me some new clothes because we didn't have enough to last us for the week. At least I could get away from my dad for a whole week. That alone was reason enough to go. I kept my apprehension to myself and as far as my parents knew, I was still elated to have the opportunity.

At the end of the week it was my turn to go. Dad drove me to the camp grounds, and I believe I had a knot in my stomach for the entire trip. As we drove onto the campground, I could see all the boys running around having fun, but David was nowhere in sight. We found his cabin, and he was inside waiting for us. Grandpa had given each of us five dollars to spend at the camp store, and my brother had bought something for everyone. My gift was a penlight, which probably ended getting more use than David had imagined. It was then time for David to leave, and for me to start my week. After kissing my family goodbye, all the girls went to orientation, then on to our cabins. I was assigned to a cabin with one of my friends from church. We made our beds and unpacked some of our belongings, and then we went off to have some fun. I was overwhelmed with all there was to do. Each day we had craft time, played games, swam, went to Bible studies and evening chapel, and still had a few hours of free time. The ice cream and snack shop was open each night, and that was where most of my five dollar allowance was spent. The Bible studies were somewhat of a challenge for me because we were given many verses to memorize. Even though I had to struggle to remember them, the verses were helpful to me.

Psa 119:11   Your word I have hidden in my heart, that I might not sin against You.

Psa 119:14   I have rejoiced in the way of Your testimonies, As *much as* in all riches.

Learning these was more than just an exercise, because God reminded me of them every time I knowingly did something I shouldn't. I often tried to shrug it off and forget what the Bible says, but I still knew that God doesn't turn a blind eye to our sin. I couldn't escape the need to repent. I had the time of my life, and it passed by much too quickly. I just hoped I would get to go again the next year.

I was far from eager to return home, partly because it had been so nice to sleep in a real bed. There were a few times when it was good to be sleeping on the sofa near my parents' bedroom door. If I became frightened or sick during the night, I could easily call out to them. But most of the time I wished my bed was someplace else. My parents never knew how hard it was for me to fall asleep. Since I slept in the sitting room, someone was constantly walking past my "bed". The television that my father eventually bought also ended up in that room. My mom went to bed much earlier than my dad, who would stay up to watch a few programs. I wasn't allowed to watch TV after I went to bed, so my mother would call out to ask if my back was turned to the television. I always did what she told me, but I had a way to circumvent their rules. I took a small mirror to bed, and held it up so that I could see the picture without anyone noticing. Since I was usually awake as late as my parents, I often overheard their conversations. I remember hearing them talk about my grades and whether or not my chores were done well. There was one conversation I wished I hadn't overheard. As my parents discussed the events of the day, my mother nonchalantly mentioned that she had redone one of my chores. She wasn't complaining; it was simply stated as a matter of fact. In response, my father asked, "Why did we have her, anyway? What good is she?" My mother's shocked reaction helped to soften the blow. "Stephen! Don't ever say that!" I knew that she loved me and was glad to have me, and looking back I believe that my father was simply burying the guilt he felt about his behavior under a cover of resentment toward me.

One benefit to my sleeping arrangement came when we had company in the evening. If they stayed late enough I would be allowed to sleep in my parents' bedroom until they went home. I was only allowed to lie across the bed, on top of the covers. I never found out why my parents enforced such a bizarre restriction.

We also had some fun outings with Grandpa. He enjoyed taking us to the amusement park on Bob Lo Island, located on the Canadian side of the Detroit River. We would hop on a bus which would take us to the ferry dock. The boat ride took about a half hour. Once we had arrived, David and I would help Grandpa carry our picnic basket, while mom carried Rick. Grandpa gave each of us five dollars to spend on rides and ice cream. Once the day was over, it was back to the boat for the return trip to Detroit. If we had money left over, we were allowed to buy a snack to eat while we listened to the band and watched people dance. Grandpa also liked to buy things for us that my parents couldn't. Wagons, bicycles, and roller-skates were just a few of the gifts he gave us.

    Another simple pleasure we enjoyed was swimming in the pool at a local park. It was about five miles from our house, and on a hot day it seemed like hours before we reached the park. We would stay there for most of the day, and then hurry home so David could deliver newspapers. One day while I was waiting to jump into the deep end, I was pushed in before I was ready and had no chance to take a breath. The water was twelve feet deep, and struggling my way to the surface seemed to take an eternity. Just as I began to emerge, I was struck on the head by a blunt object. Now I was in real trouble. Again I fought for all I was worth to get my head above water. I opened my mouth in desperation, but it was immediately filled with water instead of air. I continued to thrash frantically, hoping someone would see that I was in trouble and help me. Finally someone grabbed my hand and pulled me to the side of the pool. It was my big brother. He helped me out of the pool where I sat and coughed until I could breath properly again. Not feeling well, I laid down next to the pool. I heard a voice asking me if I was ok, and I opened my eyes to see the lifeguard standing over me. I explained what had happened, and he asked me if I knew who had pushed me. I knew that it was my friend Patricia, but I couldn't bring myself to say so. She had pushed David in right after she pushed me, and it was his heel that had hit me on the head. She didn't intend to hurt anyone, and I didn't want to get her into trouble. She lived next door, and we had become good friends. She was very kind and was a blessing to me. If I told on her, I knew that my father would not let me be her friend anymore. The last thing I wanted was to lose a friend over a simple lapse in judgment.

I caught my breath but I still wasn't feeling well, so we decided to call it a day and head home. This proved to be somewhat of a challenge when I tried to stand up. I had never had a feeling like that before. A combination of extreme dizziness and severe pain in my head made it difficult to walk. I made it to the lockers, but when I needed help getting dressed, I knew something was wrong. After telling my parents about the accident, they took me to the hospital where some x-rays were taken. They found that I had a concussion, and would need to spend the night in the hospital to make sure I'd be ok. I returned home the next day, but still did not feel normal. I felt disconnected from everything I was seeing and experiencing, as if I were an outsider observing from a distance. My head felt like it was twice its actual size. As the day passed, the feeling continued. Since my parents had gone to help clean the church, Patricia's mother took me back to the hospital. She was a great comfort to me because of her willingness to help me and pray for me. Another x-ray showed that I had a blood clot that was moving through the blood vessels. It was small enough that it didn't require any special treatment other than rest. I learned to be very careful going up and down stairs, because I experienced dizzy spells until the clot eventually dissolved. The ordeal made me wonder why God would bring me so close to death and an escape from my problems at home, then allow me to live and continue to face the turmoil.

Chapter 5

Rage

When I was 13 years old, there was a bus strike in Detroit. Since we didn't have a car at that time, Dad bought a motorbike. It served its purpose for a while, but keeping up with traffic was just too difficult for the little motor. My brothers and I had a few chances to ride on it when my father first got it, but hanging on was an exercise in futility. There was only room for one daredevil on the bike, so a passenger had to sit on the handle bars. The ride was fun until we reached top speed. Dad would head for the railroad tracks, and as soon as the front wheel made contact with what amounted to a miniature steel wall, we would be bounced high off the handlebars. After a few jarring landings we tried to tie a pillow to the handlebars, but it just kept slipping from its intended position. We quickly gave up on that idea.

Once the strike ended, dad sold the bike and went back taking the bus to work. It wasn't long before the bus drivers went on strike a second time so once again, my father had to find an affordable means of transportation. This time it was a motor scooter. It looked like a lot of fun to my brothers and me, especially since it had an extra seat for a passenger to ride behind the driver. David was allowed to ride it first, and he loved it. My turn came next, and once again I found myself flying off the thing when my father sped across the railroad tracks. Dad loved to scare me, and he did it well. His rationalization was that as long as we were afraid of him, we would do what he told us. The strike lasted for a few weeks and Dad had to make repairs to the scooter several times. Each time, he would wheel it up to the back porch and open up the hood. My brothers and I would gather around to watch him make adjustments. As we looked on during one such operation, he said to me, "Come over here on this side once and I'll show you something." He reached out to take my hand, and I reluctantly gave it to him. He touched it to the bare metal on a part of the motor that was drawing current, shocking me with a jolt of electricity. He always got a laugh from watching or causing someone else's pain and then follow up with a taunt, "You big baby…wait till next time!" After that I made sure I was nowhere in sight when he was repairing something.

Col 3:21   Fathers, do not provoke your children, lest
                  they become discouraged.

This was also the year my parents bought a television. My father and grandfather never missed a wrestling match. Of course they usually started after my bedtime, so I had to pretend to be sleeping while the two of them flinched and jumped with each maneuver of the wrestlers. My father would sit on the floor, and my grandfather sat in his creaky old chair while I hid my head under the covers to at least create the illusion of a sound barrier.

It wasn't enough for my father to simply watch wrestling matches; he had to practice the holds on someone. My brother and I were the easiest targets. Since David had a paper route I was at home more than he was, and found myself pressed against the floor more often than he did. My father would pin me with my stomach to the floor, then reach around my neck and pull my head back with his arm. If he couldn't get that right, then he would use my own arm for the choke hold. Sometimes he'd practice standing moves, which involved jerking my head one way or the other. Headaches and stiff necks became common for me. When my parents would take me to the doctor, it always raised questions as to why a thirteen year old girl needed to have her neck adjusted. I always lied and told him I didn't know. If I told the truth, I would just cause more trouble for myself. Once I was off the doctor's table, the pain was gone until the next time my dad tackled me. Maybe he would just kill me so it would finally be over. I kept wondering why he even bothered to read his Bible. It certainly didn't change him. The only verses that seemed to make their way into his head were the ones that would help him make a point or win an argument. My father had no credibility with David or me, and his scripture quotations to us fell on deaf ears.

One Wednesday night, I had a stiff neck that set off a chain of events I'll never forget. I had to finish some homework, so my parents let me stay home from our Wednesday evening church. After eating dinner and washing the dishes, David and I started working. He sat on one side of the dining table, and I sat across from him. He was always a big help to me. That evening he finished before me and went to bed. Rick had already been in bed for a while, and Grandpa was reading the newspaper in the living room. I had enough difficulty trying to finish my homework without the pain in my neck, but the challenge grew as the ache intensified. The pain eventually got so bad that I decided to call it quits and get ready for bed. The process of changing my clothes was very difficult. Raising my arms to put on my pajamas was the toughest part. Then it was time to put the sheets and blankets on the sofa. The pain brought tears to my eyes. I dropped myself to the sofa, then swung my legs onto the cushions and let my body fall back to lie down. I lay there crying until the pain eased off a bit.

It was quiet in the house. The boys were asleep and grandpa was now sitting in the kitchen. That's when it hit me – I had forgotten to make a sandwich for him. Being from the "old country", he was not accustomed to preparing food for himself. He always had a sandwich before going to bed, and since mom wasn't home it was my job to make it. I called out to him softly so I wouldn't wake my brothers. "Grandpa…I'm sorry. I forgot to make your sandwich, but my neck hurts so badly that I can't get back up."

I was sure he heard me even though he didn't respond. I repeated myself, but he retreated to his room and still refused to acknowledge my apology. I tried one last time, and then gave up. I decided I'd just explain the situation to my mom once she got home and hope for the best.

Once he was in bed, he began to mutter his complaints. "So that's it. Just go off to bed and leave me sitting waiting for my sandwich."

I knew I was going to be in big trouble. I called out to him a few times to tell him that my mother would fix him some food as soon as she came home. It didn't mean a thing to him…his grumbling continued. I began to pray that things wouldn't escalate too much. "Please Lord, help me" was my simple request. Maybe things will be alright since my parents are coming home from church.

It was about 10:30 when I heard he old car coming down the alley. I knew it would only be a few short minutes before mom would hear him and the trouble would start. I had each step of her routine mapped out in my mind. Once out of the car, she would come into the back yard then unlock the garage door and turn on the light. Next she would go to the back of the garage, unlock the big doors, push one open, then the other. She would place a brick in front of each door to hold it back for my father to park the car. Then she would be on her way toward the house and up to the back door.

She opened the door to be greeted by the grievance my grandfather was broadcasting from his bedroom. She immediately went to his room and let him know that she heard him, and would get him a sandwich. On her way to hang up her coat, she stopped at the side of my bed. My heart was pounding. "Sis", she said, "what is going on? Why didn't you make grandpa something to eat?"

The trouble was starting. Once again I repeated what I had told my grandfather about my neck. Mom said she'd go tell grandpa that she would make him a sandwich and serve him in bed. She thought he would like that and it would stop his complaining.

Now my father's steps were running through my mind. He's probably done parking the car. Next he'll be walking to the back of the garage, stepping into the alley to remove the bricks from alongside of the doors. Now he's pulled the doors shut, and has begun the walk to the house.

As my father entered the house, my mother was in the kitchen preparing food for my grandfather who was still in his bedroom complaining. Dad's reaction was the polar opposite of my mother's. I had been hoping that a miracle would happen and he would ignore his father. Things didn't quite work out that way. He hurried over to the bedroom door, which was at the side of the dining room. In a hushed, but obviously irritated tone he asked my grandfather, "What are you belly aching about this time?"

Hearing the exasperation in his son's voice and finally realizing the trouble he was about to cause for everyone, Grandpa answered yieldingly, "Nothing. Just nothing."

My dad raised his voice, no longer concerned with waking my brothers. "Well we will just see about that!" He marched from the dining room and appeared instantly beside the sofa where I lay. He looked down at me and said, "Well, what do you have to say for yourself?"

Yet again I explained what happened from the beginning, but it didn't faze my dad. "Just wait until I get back! I'll fix you but good", he promised.

I knew what that meant, and immediately I began to beg, "Oh God, please help me!"

I continued to pray as my father left to hang up his overcoat in the front hall closet. "Please make this go away".

I had a sinking feeling in my stomach as I watched him take off his suit coat and walk over to my bed. He grabbed me by the head, stood me on my feet in front of him, and barked, "I'll show you what a stiff neck is all about!"

With that, he jerked my head to the right, then to the left. He let go of me, and I crumpled to my knees in pain. As I slowly pulled myself up to the sofa, I heard him yell at his father, "I'm going to fix you, old man! I'm sick of your complaining about everything!" He headed back through the dining room and into Grandpa's bedroom.

"Oh God, please! Where are you? Please don't let him kill Grandpa."

As Dad entered Grandpa's room, he kicked the old clothes iron that propped the door open. It skidded across the floor and came to a stop under the bed. My father stormed in the same direction and began shouting at my grandfather. "Now what are you complaining about?!"

Grandpa realized that he'd already said too much and

would have to try his best to appease his son. He told my father he was sorry for the trouble he had caused. "I don't need anything to eat. I'll be ok."

During all the commotion, my brothers woke up and came to the bedroom door. Our mother was standing at Dad's side, trying her best to calm him down. "Stephen, please! He said he was sorry", she reminded him. "Please don't do anything. Just let him alone." He acted as if he didn't hear a word she spoke and kept on yelling and cursing at my grandfather.

Grandpa continued to apologize. "Son, I'm sorry. It won't happen again. I'll move out if that's what you want."

I joined my brothers as they observed from the doorway, and we watched in disbelief at the scene unfolding before us. As we looked on, my father suddenly reached his boiling point and lunged at our grandfather. "I've had enough of you! I'm going to kill you!"

My mother yelled, "Stephen! Stephen, don't do this! Oh, God...Stephen!" Again my father ignored her pleas for mercy, and grabbed my grandfather by his union suit, the long underwear he wore year round. He was a frail man who was only 5'4" tall and weighed about 115 pounds. The rest of us retreated from the door as he pulled my grandfather out of his bed and shouted, "Come on, old man! You're coming with me!"

My thoughts turned to the rifle my dad owned and the bullets he kept in his dresser drawer. I had seen them many times when I put away my parents' clothing that I had ironed. I told David to sneak into the room, grab the bullets and run next door with them. My dad seemed to be blinded by his rage, and by God's grace David was able to get out of the house without being seen. He went next door to Patricia's house, and her mother answered the door. She let him inside, and he asked if he could use the phone to call our pastor for prayer. I was hoping he would call the police, but that may have just brought us more trouble in the future. David returned to the house just in time to see our dad dragging grandpa from the dining room into the sitting room, then past my bed and into our parents' bedroom. He continued to yell, "I'll kill you old man! You won't make trouble around here anymore!"

My grandfather begged for his life. "Stephen, Stephen! Please! Please, I won't cause anymore trouble. Son, I'll leave. I'll leave you alone. I won't say anymore. Just let me go."

My mom continued to beg my dad to stop, and my brothers and I fell to our knees beside my bed and cried out to the Lord for help. As we began to pray, my dad picked up his father and threw him across the room. My grandfather hit the bed with enough force to knock it against the far wall. Dad grabbed him again and pulled him toward the closet where he kept his rifle. With one hand he hung onto my grandfather, and with the other he reached into the closet and retrieved his gun. David, Rick, and I were too scared to stay on our knees for long, and sought protection behind our mother. We cried and begged him to let grandpa go. He didn't hear a word we said. He dragged Grandpa around the bed, and over to the dresser. He propped the rifle against the dresser, opened the top drawer to search for his bullets. He looked at the drawer with disbelief when he couldn't find them, and began pulling all of the contents out and tossing them about the room. "Where are they?! Who took them?!" My mom had no idea that David had hidden them.

It dawned on me that Dad didn't realize the boys were even out of bed. I turned and told them to get into bed right away before Dad saw them and started asking questions about the bullets. They listened to my advice, ran off to bed and hid under the covers pretending to be asleep and oblivious to the violence in the next room.

Frustrated by the mysterious absence of his bullets, my father finally let go of Grandpa and walked out of the room, passing my mother and me. He looked at me as he exited the room, and I couldn't believe what I saw. His pupils were so dilated that it completely changed his appearance, and it scared me even beyond the fear I already felt. I froze in the spot beside my bed, right where all of this had started just a few minutes earlier. He never said a word, but went through the living room and into the front closet for his overcoat, which he had worn to church earlier that evening. He put it on, and then went out of the house and down the steps. We had no idea where he was headed.

My mom told Grandpa to go to bed and try to put this behind him. He walked past and said, "I'm sorry, Janeen.

I'm sorry, Verna."

Mom told him that it was okay, and she was sorry too. "Just go to bed and try to sleep." He could hardly walk after being thrown around by my father. As he left room, my brothers got out of bed again and wanted to know what was going on. Mom told them that she didn't know, and that my father had just left without saying a word. She asked us if we knew what had happened to the bullets, and David told her that he had taken them next door and would retrieve them the next day. She told David and Rick not to say anything about it to their father, but she didn't have to. They already knew what would happen if he found out.

My mom told the boys to go to bed, and then it was my turn to hear from her. My heart was beating so hard and so fast that I could hear it in my ears. I wasn't prepared for what I was about to hear. She looked at me and said, "This is all your fault. You know that?! Go to bed."

I went back to the bed crying, and struggled to lie down again. Mom went back into the kitchen to put some dishes away and went to bed without another word. I lay in my bed wondering what I could have done differently. I didn't get much sleep that night. With my bed in the middle of the house, it was inevitable that my dad would be passing by within inches of me as he went to his room. I thought of my prayers from earlier that evening, and tried to imagine a reason why God didn't answer. He could have stopped all of it from happening, but didn't. He seemed to be watching all of the events of my life with indifference. Deep down I was still convinced that God did love me and cared about what was happening to me and my family. The only way I could reconcile God's love with his apparent inaction was to recognize that the source of my problems was my father's sin rather than God's apathy. If my father truly loved God, none of this would be happening. I concluded that my dad must not really be a Christian. He just knew a lot about the Bible, and how to act the part when he was at church. Two verses in particular seemed perfectly applicable to my father's charade:

1Jo 1:6   If we say that we have fellowship with Him, and walk in darkness, we lie and do not practice the truth.

1Jo 2:4   He who says, "I know Him," and does not keep His commandments, is a liar, and the truth is not in him.

I knew that Satan will do everything he can to destroy a Christian. The fact that my father was not a true believer made him the perfect accomplice in an apparent attempt to prevent me from becoming a strong Christian woman who would raise a family that would serve the Lord.

After a couple of hours of lying in bed thinking and praying, I heard my dad at the front door. Fear welled up inside of me, not knowing if the whole mess would start over again. Where had he been for the last two hours? None of us ever found out. Now that he's back, what is he going to do to us…or me? I waited for him to hang up his coat and listened for every motion and every step. I heard him coming my way, and my mind raced to determine the best course of action. Do I pretend to be asleep, or try to apologize? Maybe I should just wait and hope he goes to straight to bed. He walked past the boys' bedroom and through the living room. He entered the room where I slept and stopped there for the longest second I've ever endured. I hoped he couldn't tell I was crying, and I tried to remain perfectly still. Finally, and to my relief, he turned and went into his bedroom without speaking a word.

The next day came and none of us mentioned what had happened the night before. At first, we were all walking on eggshells for fear that we would set off Dad's temper again. None of us even felt free to speak when he was around. Gradually, we began to relax and feel a bit more comfortable talking. For the first few days after the incident, Dad just sat at the dinner table very quietly. It didn't take him long to return to his nasty, sarcastic self. The rest of us knew better than to speak with even a hint of disrespect. It was a double standard he strictly enforced.

Once again, it was more than his mean spirited comments that were a threat. His hands were always where they shouldn't be. They looked so ugly to me. Every time he grabbed or groped me I would plead with him to stop, but he'd never yield. Taking a bath was always a battle of wits between my father and me. Once I went into the bathroom, he would shout through the door "Don't you lock that door! We know you're in there."

He would try to come in every time, and no matter what I

was doing he either wanted to watch or help. If I was using the toilet, he would just stand there and watch. If I was taking a bath, he would say "Let me wash your back".

I always kept a towel at arms length so I could grab it and cover myself if he walked in. He loved to torment me. Sometimes he would throw a glass of cold water on me, soaking the towel I used to cover myself. Of course that wasn't enough, so he would yank the towel away from me and toss it into the bathwater. Then he'd laugh and ask, "Why don't you have anything to cover up?"

Somehow he could do all these things and still tell me never to let a date touch me because the Bible says we are to wait until marriage. I never dared to ask him why it was ok for him to do it.

I finally had enough and decided to start locking the door, no matter what my father said. It had an old fashioned lock and keyhole, and it was opened with a large key that we would leave in the keyhole so we wouldn't misplace it. Once I started locking the door, my dad decided to show me how silly I was to try to keep him out. When he was sure I had gotten into the tub, he'd slide a piece of paper on the floor until it was halfway under the door. Next he'd use a nut cracker pick to push the key out of the lock. It would fall onto the paper, enabling him to pull the paper back under the door along with the key. All he had to do then was unlock the door and he was in.

In my next attempt to attain some privacy, I removed the

key from the keyhole after I locked the door. That didn't work either, because my father would simply press his face to the door and look right through the keyhole at me. I tried stuffing a wad of paper in the keyhole, but he would immediately push it back out and laugh at me. My dresser was kept in the bathroom because we didn't have enough room for it anywhere else in the house, and it actually provided another option for me. I pushed it in front of the door, which prevented him from opening the door even if he had the key and it blocked his view from the keyhole. His only option was to push the door hard enough to knock the dresser over, or so I thought.

Feeling secure with my newest plan, I sat warm and happy in the tub when I heard his caustic laugh. I couldn't figure out where it was coming from until I looked around the room and saw that menacing face of his staring at me from the window. I grabbed my towel, threw it around myself and jumped out of the tub. Then I took another out of the cupboard and tried over and over again to throw it over the curtain rod while he peered in and laughed at me. Catching glances of his face as I tried to block the window gave me such a sick feeling in the pit of my stomach that I wanted to die. I began to cry, and the harder I cried, the harder he laughed.

From that day on I had a new routine for taking a bath. Walk into the bathroom, close the door, put a towel over the curtain rod, then move the dresser in front of the door. All of that effort was just to take a bath in privacy.

Again I prayed, "Dear father in Heaven, don't you care? Do all fathers do these things? I'm so tired of trying to hide from him. Tired of having teeth marks on my backside and pinch marks on my chest. So tired of having sore, heavy arms from having them twisted behind my head or straight out in front of me. And for what reason? Just to hear me say 'uncle'?! Lord, I say it before he even starts but he just likes to see us in pain. Will this ever end?"

I reminded God of what His word said in the 56th chapter of Psalms.

Psa 56:8 You number my wanderings;
Put my tears into Your bottle;
Are they not in Your book?

Chapter 6

Leila

When I was fourteen, a girl named Leila and her family moved into a house just a few doors away from ours. At first I thought it was great, and I was happy to have a friend that was allowed to come over at any time. She would even go to church with us, and eventually claimed that she had accepted Jesus as her savior.

I would go to her house occasionally, but most of the time she wanted to come to my house. After a while I realized that it was because of all the attention she was receiving from my dad.

Leila revealed her devious side one afternoon while I was at her house. "Do you like grape juice?" she asked.

As silly as it may seem, the opportunity to have even a small taste of grape juice was one of the reasons I enjoyed taking communion. I loved grape juice, but my parents never bought it. Leila explained that her grandmother makes juice for her family. She went to the cupboard and brought out a large glass, followed by a bottle of her grandmother's home-made juice. I was overjoyed as she poured it because I had never had my own glass of grape juice before. I should have known something was wrong when she didn't pour any for herself. I took a few big gulps, and then lowered the glass while Leila stared at me with a blank look on her face. The flavor wasn't what I expected, and my face showed it.

"What's the matter?" Leila asked.

"Is this wine or vinegar?" I replied.

"No, it's grape juice! What do you think it is?"

"Like I said…it's either wine or vinegar."

"No it's not. You're going to hurt my grandmother's feelings if you don't drink it."

Her grandmother didn't speak English, and had no idea what we were saying. She just smiled at us. I told Leila that I needed to go home, and she insisted on coming along. As we walked toward my house, I became very dizzy and had a hard time walking in a straight line. Leila began to laugh at me and she asked why I was having so much trouble walking. That was the last clue I needed to be sure she had given me bad wine. I had never tasted alcohol before.

I had to think fast about which way to enter the house. I decided to go in through the front door because my father would probably be sitting in the kitchen. I opened the door and let Leila enter first, so my parents would start talking to her and wouldn't pay attention to what I was doing. My mom and dad were sitting at the kitchen table, and began talking to Leila when we made our way to the back of the house. I slipped away to rinse my mouth with mouthwash and find a piece of gum I could chew to hide the smell of alcohol. Then

I simply stayed out of sight until the effects of the wine had worn off.

I knew Leila would never get the blame for what she had done. My dad liked her, and made no attempts to hide it. After he came home from work, Leila would wander over to our house and make herself at home. During one of her visits, my dad invited her to spend the night. She quickly took him up on his offer, and ran home to get her things. While she was gone, I listened to my dad telling me what a nice girl she was. When Leila returned, my dad treated her to some chocolate candy, and I was told to open up the sofa bed so both of us would have a place to sleep. In the morning, Leila went home and it was my responsibility to make up the bed by myself. This got old very quickly, but complaining to my mom about all that was going on was useless. She had already talked to my dad about Leila, and he got angry with her. When Leila slept over, it was about the only time I was allowed to unfold the sofa bed. It made me wonder once again why I couldn't unfold it for myself. At least then I would fall off the sofa in the middle of the night. Then again, if I opened it up the mattress would be lower to the ground and I wouldn't be quite as accessible for my dad.

Dad tried to find candy for Leila each time she came over. Occasionally he would give her just a few pieces of candy, which she was more than happy to eat in front of me. She would make remarks about how wonderful my dad was, and how she wished he was her dad. The funny thing was, so did I. Having met her dad, I thought she must be crazy. He was a very tall and nice looking man. He was soft-spoken and hard working. When I really took a look at Leila, I knew why my dad liked her. She was very cute and more endowed than me. Of course she would talk and flirt with him to perpetuate the special treatment. Kids at school began to ask me if the things Leila was saying were true. She told them about the candy and money my dad gave her, and the kisses he greeted her with. The only thing I could say was "Yep. It's all true."

One day our supply of chocolate had run out, so dad sent me to the Sander's candy store four blocks away. He told me to get two pounds of candy kisses – one pound for himself, and one pound for Leila. I thought that since I was the one who had to make the trip to the store by myself, maybe some of the candy would be for me and my brothers. When I returned with the candy he took one box, and told me that the other was for Leila. My dad left the room with his candy, and never uttered a word of thanks for going to the store for him. My next thought was that maybe Leila would share hers with us, but she soon made an excuse to go home early so she could have it all to herself.

The next day at school, the ball finally dropped as we were lined up next to the blackboard waiting for the last bell to ring. Leila announced to the class that my dad liked her much better than he liked me. Even though that thought had been in the back of my mind for quite some time, I couldn't believe I was hearing her actually say it. She went on to tell them about the candy my father gave her, and even bragged that she never gave me one piece. For her to tell it to all of my classmates was incredibly hurtful, and I made up my mind to talk it over with my mom one more time.

Before Leila came over that evening, mom and I had a talk with dad. Even my brother had heard about the incident. My dad actually listened as I recounted the day's events, and realized that Leila was making fools out of all of us. I went a step further and told him that even I believed he loved her more than me. It was one of the few times he realized he had made a mistake. When I finished telling my side of the story, he replied "Can I ask her with you standing here if she really said that?"

"Sure", I said. "You can even ask the other kids in my class if you want to."

Of course he didn't do that, since he already looked silly for letting a young girl use him. He didn't want to get into trouble with her parents, so he knew he needed to put a stop to it. When Leila came over that evening, he told her that he was unhappy with what she had done at school. She listened to what he had to say, then suddenly came up with a reason to go home early. After that evening Leila never came back to our house, and her family moved away just a few months later.

Once Leila was out of my life, the problems with my dad began again. Every night when I went to bed, I would curl up into the fetal position to make myself less accessible to my dad. When I was sure I'd be left alone for the night, the memories of the day would start replaying in my mind and I would often cry myself to sleep. For comfort I would read my Bible. In my prayers I recited Psalm 10, verses 12-15:

Psa 10:12	Arise, O LORD! O God, lift up Your hand! Do not forget the humble.
Psa 10:13	Why do the wicked renounce God? He has said in his heart, "You will not require *an account.*"
Psa 10:14	But You have seen, for You observe trouble and grief, to repay *it* by Your hand. The helpless commits himself to You; You are the helper of the fatherless.
Psa 10:15	Break the arm of the wicked and the evil *man;* Seek out his wickedness *until* You find none.

Chapter 7

Family Vacations

During the early 1950's, my mother began working at our church. Being the janitor was not a glamorous job, but she felt blessed to be making some money. Finances were always tight at our house, and there was rarely enough food on the dinner table. At night, pangs of hunger would keep me awake, so I would creep out of bed and quietly go into the pantry to get a slice of bread. It was just enough to help me fall asleep. With the additional income from my mom's job, there was more food on the table and more clothing on our backs. We were even able to buy a car. It was old, but it got us to and from church.

With my mom working, I was given additional responsibilities. It was my job to get dinner started. I'd peel potatoes, wash vegetables, and set the table. If mom wasn't home by a certain time, I was to turn on the stove and start cooking. Other times, before I left for school, I would be told where to find some money when I got home and which groceries to buy for dinner that evening. It was a long walk from our house to the stores where we did most of our shopping. On the way I passed the foundry and the huge sand piles on the next block where we played. We were often chased out for our own safety by the same man who gave my grandfather scraps of wood to keep us warm in the winter. He brought them home in the wagon he built for my brothers and me, and then he would cut it into smaller pieces to be taken into the basement. Once he had brought it all inside, he would cut it again into pieces small enough to fit into the furnace. Every once in a while as I walked by, the man would be standing at the foundry's loading dock where the large trucks brought deliveries of wood. Always friendly, he would smile and ask how we were all doing.

As I continued to the store, I crossed the railroad tracks that my grandfather had laid on while drunk and depressed. It was wonderful to know how much he had changed since he had put his faith in Christ. One set of the tracks ran to the foundry, and another ran into the scrap yard across the street. There were four or five sets of tracks there, and crossing them could be quite challenging at times. They were heavily traveled by trains filled with goods of all kinds, livestock, new cars, heavy equipment, and passengers. When I saw a train approaching, I'd race to get across all the tracks without having to wait for it to pass. There were a few times when I almost didn't make it. Just hearing the incredible weight of the machine rolling over the tracks and the warning blast from the whistle was enough to freeze my feet to the ground. I kept trying, though. What did I have to lose? Nothing but the fear I faced at home and the pain in my stomach. Sometimes I would make it across one set of tracks before the train reached me, just to be stopped by another one I couldn't outrun. One train passed on the set of tracks in front of me as another rolled on behind me. I'd stand there shivering and the people on board waved to me as they flew by. I always wondered where they were going and what their lives were like. I wished I could find out. The dining car was where I wanted to be. Maybe someday.

After the train had cleared in front of me, I'd continue past the General Motors Ternsted division. When my dad was young, it was a field of wildflowers where he and his mother would make daisy chains. The plant produced parts for cars and trucks and for military vehicles during WWII. Across the street and on the next block were more houses. Once I reached the church at the end of the street (it was the same one my brother and I were asked to leave) I would turn right to cross the street and finally arrive at the A&P store to shop.

After taking a shopping cart, my first stop was the candy aisle just to make sure there were no open bags of candy. If there was one, I'd have to try one or to just to find out whether or not I liked it. I never did find one I didn't like. The next stop was the meat counter. My parents were creatures of habit, so it was always the same order: half a round steak, cubed twice. I was also allowed to buy lunch meat now that mom was working. It was something we could never afford until then. Moving on to the vegetable aisle, I'd pick up a can of red kidney beans then continue to the checkout counter. On weekends I would have to go another two blocks to the Sander's bakery and candy store for half of a caramel cake or half of a chocolate bump cake.

Once my shopping was done and I was on my way home, the challenge to beat the trains lay ahead of me again. Should I try to outrun it? No way! Not on the way back. I knew I'd never make it with the groceries I was carting around. I couldn't afford to risk breaking the paper bag and dropping our dinner, so I was always more cautious on the way home.

We all got a break from our responsibilities when my parents decided to take us on our first real vacation. My mother had been corresponding with her cousin, Edna, for years but we had never been to Wisconsin to visit her. Occasionally she would bring her three daughters to visit us in Detroit. We loved seeing them and hearing the stories about their town. Edna was a very good seamstress, and made most of her daughters' clothing, including their wedding dresses. When she found out that I needed clothes, she sent large boxes of them for me. Edna always sent us a letter to let us know that a package was on its way. I'd run home from school everyday to see if it had arrived.

One day we received a letter asking us if we would come to visit her. She had always been the one to travel, and she thought it would be nice for us to see where they lived. We accepted her invitation, and planned our trip. With six of us stuffed into our very old car, one of us was constantly getting an elbow in the ribs, prodding us to move over. Each of us took turns sitting in the front seat with mom and dad, giving us a chance to have some breathing room. It was very hot that day. We got lost on the way there, but eventually arrived with everyone in one piece and relatively happy. The day got much better as we settled in and began to enjoy being out in the country. It was wonderful to finally see their house, and all the food that they had brought out for us. They prepared roast beef, home grown corn, green beans, and tomatoes. We even had dessert. After dinner, we all sang a hymn together and said a prayer for everyone in the family. Everything was going very well, even for Grandpa who was getting to know Edna's father, John. They were around the same age, both being in their seventies. Later that night, Edna gave us milk and homemade cookies before we went to bed. As I was lying in bed, I could hear their conversation about the family and the Lord. I listened to my father talk about God and the Bible, and wondered whether or not he actually believed the things he was saying.

Our second day ended with some excitement. My cousins and brothers and I had just gone to bed, but had stayed awake talking for a little while. Colleen interrupted the flow of our conversation. "I hear something in the room", she whispered urgently. "Listen and be quiet for a minute."

All of a sudden she let out a loud scream, jumped out of bed, and started running down the hall, yelling "There's a bat in my hair! Get him out! Get him out!"

I followed after her, and as we were running around the dining room table her mom and dad told her to go outside to give the bat a chance to get loose and fly away. If that didn't happen, they would cut her hair off to untangle it. The last thing she wanted was for her beautiful, long blonde hair to be cut. She ran out the door and down the steps with all of us following right behind her. Colleen and the bat were both screeching loud enough to be heard a mile away. As she ran, she shook her head from side to side until the bat came loose and flew away still squealing like a car in need of new brake pads.

I remember that vacation for more than just the bat, though. Seeing the wonderful home life she had, and getting to know her well made me feel comfortable enough to open up to her. I began to tell her about what my life was like, and about the things my father had been doing. I begged her not to tell anyone because my dad would punish me even more. She was shocked to hear my stories, and couldn't understand how my father could do those things and still call himself a Christian.

I knew what her first question would be. "Why doesn't your mom do something?!"

I explained that my mother had tried to stop him, but then he just turns on her. Colleen wanted me to go to the police, but I told her that it would just bring more trouble. Even if they were to arrest him, he would eventually come home and beat me even more.

The last full day we were there, Aunt Edna asked if I could stay for a few weeks. My mom thought it would be ok, but didn't know how I would get home. Edna told her not to worry about that…she would see to it that I got home before the school year started. My mom said that I would need to ask my dad. Always suspicious, he first asked why she wanted me to stay, then how I would get home. Edna explained again that she thought it would be nice for Colleen and me to spend more time together, and that it would be no problem for them to bring me home in time for school.

I think that was when a light went on in my father's head. He looked at me, then looked back at Edna, and simply said "No."

My heart sank and I felt sick inside, fearing that he was going to grill me about what I had said to my cousin. I decided that if my father started asking me about my conversations with Colleen, I would just lie. I felt so safe with my cousins, and we had so much fun together. We had run through the cornfields and walked to town to watch a movie on the side of a building. There was always more than enough food on the table, and we even got to go out for ice cream. The five days we spent there gave me an incredible hunger for a normal home life. After everyone else fell asleep that night, I cried out to God for mercy and protection from my father.

Saying goodbye the next day was made even more difficult by the uncertainty of my fate once we were out of sight. We hadn't gone too many miles when from the front seat I heard the words I had been dreading. "Well Janeen, what did you say to them to make them want you to stay?"

Mom jumped in and said, "It's a normal thing for girls to want to spend time with each other. Maybe someday Colleen could come and stay with us for a week or so."

To my relief, that was a sufficient explanation (and diversion) and no more was said. However, I was never allowed to visit my cousins again. The next summer, my parents planned another trip to Wisconsin, but they told me that I would be staying home with my grandfather. I couldn't believe it. Why should I be the one to stay home instead of my brothers since my cousin is a girl? As soon as the question entered my mind, the answer followed. "Of course…my dad doesn't want me talking to Colleen or Edna about the abuse. The fact that he doesn't get along with Grandpa gives him an excuse to make me stay home."

My parents knew that I was a good housekeeper and a big help to Grandpa. I had proven myself invaluable to him one summer afternoon while mom was working. I was at home cleaning and watching television and my brothers were out delivering papers. It had been a beautiful day, but with one glance out the window I could see that things were changing in a hurry. I went to the basement door and called down to my grandfather. "Grandpa! There's a thunderstorm coming. You'd better shut off the tools."

He answered, "Aye. I hear ye girl." And went right back to his work.

I didn't want to take any chances, so I turned off the TV and shut all the windows. Just a few minutes later, the thunder and lightning struck with a vengeance and scared the life out of me. I noticed that my grandfather's table saw fell silent, and I remember thinking "Oh, good…he decided to shut everything down. The thunder must have startled him, too."

I hoped that the boys found shelter on someone's porch because the storm was surprisingly violent. I sat down by the window to watch the rain and lightning, and heard the water running in the bathroom. I assumed that grandpa was just washing his hands after quitting for the day, so I stayed where

I was until I heard him call for me. "Lass, could you get me some Band-Aids?"

"Sure", I said. "I'm coming."

As I entered the bathroom I saw grandpa sitting on the edge of the bathtub holding his left hand under cold running water in the sink. I took a few steps forward to see what he had done and all I could see was blood pouring out from his fingers.

"Grandpa, we need to turn off the water and see how badly you're injured."

"Just give me the bandages girl, and I'll be ok."

I insisted on taking a closer look. Once the water was off, I could see that he needed a doctor right away. The table saw had cut a diagonal gash starting near the tip of his middle finger and ending near the base of his little finger. Fortunately the storm had died down and my brothers had just come in through the back door. They spotted grandpa and me in the bathroom and came to see what was happening. I knew David would panic if he saw all the blood, so I asked him to get a belt to use as a tourniquet while I wrapped a towel around my grandfather's hand. We got out the phonebook and found a doctor who was within walking distance of our house. The boys got a blanket and placed it in the wagon so we could wheel grandpa to the office.

How strange we must have looked, three kids pulling an elderly man down the sidewalk in a wagon. We traveled four blocks west and up a tall flight of stairs without him passing out from blood loss. We told the nurse what had happened, and she told us to come right in with him. She took the towel from his hand and when she saw how badly he had been cut, she praised us for the way we had handled the situation. Grandpa had almost lost three of his fingers which ended up being held together by forty five stitches.

Since my mom was working every day, I took care of Grandpa while he recovered. I even cleaned his false teeth for him. The time we spent together then drew us closer. He knew I wanted to be a nurse, and I remember him saying "Aye, gal. You will make a fine nurse some day."

When my parents were in Wisconsin, I also had to take on David's paper route for the week. I didn't mind learning the route because it included Fort Wayne, where soldiers were stationed. It was a very nice place to walk around, and all I had to do was drop off the papers. I didn't have to do the collecting; David would do that when he got home. I also knew that he would pay me generously for filling in for him, and my parents would also pay me for taking care of Grandpa and the house. Earning some money made it eased my disappointment in not being allowed to go to Wisconsin, and either way I was getting a break from my father.

The week didn't go by without incident, though. I had become friends with a girl who lived next door named Patricia, and one day she asked if she could spend the night at our house. Since my parents were away and my grandfather liked Patricia, she was allowed to stay. We had a new sofa that opened out to a double bed, and it accommodated us nicely. After we awoke the next morning, Patricia and I lay talking about typical interests of fifteen year old girls when I heard my brother's dog begin to bark. I had let him out the night before but forgot to let him in. Rex was a big, friendly boxer. I didn't want grandpa to wake up and interrupt our conversation, so I quickly went to the back door to let him in. I made him stay in his corner of the kitchen, and then hurried back to the living room and sat back down on the bed. Rex wasn't happy just being in the house, though. He came running into the living room, took a leap, and ended up colliding with my face. His teeth hit mine, shattering the crown that concealed the dead root in the front and center of my smile. Once again, all that remained in its place was a fragment of a tooth that looked like a small nail. When I took a look at it in the mirror, all I could think was "Now what?!"

I collected my thoughts and made a call to Wisconsin to let my parents know what had happened. I spoke with my mom, and her response wasn't much of a surprise. "Well, there's not much that can be done until we get home."

It wasn't exactly a life threatening situation, so my parents continued their vacation as planned. I was sure that I'd be in big trouble when they came home, but I got a big surprise. As soon as they got home, they began calling around to find a dentist that would take care of it right away. In just a few days, my tooth was back to normal and I was feeling much better about myself.

Over the course of the next year, tensions between my father and grandfather began to ease, and we all started to go on vacations together. We went to northern Michigan and spent a whole week in a log cabin at Houghton Lake. Dad would get up at four in the morning to go fishing, and mom was the only one willing to go with him. In the afternoon of our first day, we went berry picking. Mom had bought a shiny metal bucket for each of us before the trip. There wasn't a farm nearby, but there were plenty of berries hiding in the woods. My parents went searching in one direction, and my brothers and I went the other. My mother was farthest from us, and after a while we heard my dad call to her in a calm but firm voice, "Verna…don't say a word, but just move toward me and keep coming."

We looked beyond our dad to see what was wrong, and saw that my mom was standing just a few yards from a mother bear and her two cubs. As mom slowly made her way over to the rest of us, we all got out of the woods as quickly as we could without drawing the bear's attention to us. That wasn't our only wildlife encounter. We didn't want to give up on finding berries, so we went back to the woods a couple of days later. Mom was a few feet away when she said, "Kids, there's a snake here. Don't move fast, just move back slowly and don't take your eyes off it."

The snake was an Eastern Mississauga Rattlesnake – the only venomous snake native to Michigan. It was about two feet long, and had a thick, dark brown body covered with a light brown pattern that resembled chain links. Its head was raised, its tongue was flickering, and its tail was rattling. We backed away from the snake, and it uncoiled and sped away in the opposite direction. Mom and dad never went back into the woods and told us not to go without them. We went back a few times anyway. We decided that what our parents didn't know wouldn't hurt them, and we would be careful and watch out for each other.

One morning when my parents left for a fishing trip, they decided to wear their bathing suits on the boat. It had been a very warm night, and they planned on returning before noon. My brothers and I would go down to the edge of the water and watch for them until they came to the dock, then we would help bring their gear back to the house. As they came into sight on this particular day, I couldn't believe my eyes. My mom was as red as a beet. She had never spent so much time in the sun wearing only a bathing suit, and had suffered severe sunburn. As the day wore on, she began to run a fever and got the chills. It was the end of the vacation for her; she spent the next three days in bed. My father had taken first aid classes as part of the training for his job at Detroit Edison, and it was apparent to him that my mother had second degree burns. They covered her back, shoulders, part of her chest, and the front of her legs. By the next day her burns began to blister, and she was eventually covered with a layer of dead, white skin. We kept cool, damp cloths on her and tried to make her as comfortable as possible.

We all felt sorry for mom because she really needed vacations. She worked very hard at the church for the modest pay she received. We would help her whenever we could. Sometimes I would go out to the church and surprise her, and she was always grateful for the help. The church was being renovated to accommodate the growing congregation, and there weren't enough people to remove concrete and lay tile. Mom and dad had become devoted members of the church, so they worked hard every Saturday to finish the job. During the week, mom laid tile so there would be one more classroom ready for Sunday school. Except for the time she ended up with second degree sunburns, getting away from our daily routine was a great chance for her to relax. It also led my brothers and me to think that our lives might be getting better since we had such fun, trouble free time.

With our vacation over and autumn quickly approaching, it seemed like I was the only sixteen year old who wasn't eagerly anticipating the start of a new school year. As the days wore on, I became more and more aware of my stomach problems worsening with pain and constant diarrhea. My periods had begun at age 14, and I always ended up in bed for a day each month because of them. We didn't have enough money for proper protection, so I had several embarrassing moments. It was the last bit of motivation I needed to decide to get a job.

I started babysitting for a neighbor, and learned to weave potholders that I sold to our neighbors. David was generous with the money he earned from his paper route, and always tried to help me. His customers tipped him well, because he was likeable and did a good job. He often saved his extra earnings until he had enough to buy something for Rick or me. Every once in a while, David gave me money to buy something at the dime store that I could resell at a higher price. I also learned to sew well enough to make stuffed elephants. To maximize my profit, I stuffed the elephants with sawdust from my grandfather's workshop in our basement. Our entrepreneurial ventures allowed us to afford both essentials and nonessentials that we would never have had otherwise.

Chapter 8

The Best Laid Plans...

David and I relied on each other for comfort. We would talk about our lives as we walked along the railroad tracks on our way to school. David never seemed to have a moment of optimism. He seemed to only seek comfort in thoughts of suicide. On one of our walks to school he told me once again that he wanted to die, and then stepped up onto the rail. He steadied himself, and continued to walk on the steel that began to vibrate in response to the approaching train. He said, "Watch how close the train will come before I jump off."

I was frightened that he might not jump off at all. I knew how desperately he wanted to be free from the torment, and that death (either his or my father's) was the only deliverance he could imagine. He made nooses out of string and drew the familiar stick-figure hanged man in his notebooks. "Someday I'll do it" he'd say.

"If you don't stop it, I'm not going to walk to school with you anymore", I warned. He didn't like to go anywhere by himself if he didn't have to, so my threat was enough to persuade him to step down from the track.

David was a good hearted person, and I loved him very much. Sometimes his judgment was clouded by his desire to help others. He occasionally brought home fresh vegetables for our dinner, since my father couldn't afford enough food. At first he told us he bought them, but eventually admitted stealing them from the loading dock at the cold storage warehouse where trains stopped to make deliveries. He was caught by one of the workers, but when David explained himself, the man gave him a paper bag and told him he could fill it with anything that fell on the ground. David also bought things for Rick and me. He had a short white jacket that the two of us liked a lot. It had elastic around the waist, a pocket on each side, and one chest pocket to the left of the zipper. The collar had to be turned up in the back if you really wanted to be fashionable. Without any need for a special occasion, he took me to the store and bought me a jacket just like his and later did the same for Rick. There were plenty of other times when David took us roller skating, ice skating, or swimming. The only thing I was able to do in return was try to console him when he felt hopeless. When my parents were eating in the kitchen before going to bed, David would sneak out of his room to come talk to me. We usually had about 20 minutes before my parents would finish up and walk through my room to go to bed. My brother would pour out his heart to me, but comforting him was next to impossible and it began to create a rift between us. I was trying to serve the Lord as well as I could, but David was unable to see how God could love us and still let these things happen to us. He became rebellious, and I found myself telling lies to keep him and Rick out of trouble. David would skip classes and get Rick out of school. I often found out about it, and would administer my own punishment which amounted to little more than blackmail. We made a deal. I would not tell our parents if he cleaned and shined my shoes for a month.

After this happened a few times, I began to feel guilty. I confronted David one more time. "This is wrong. You are leading our little brother into doing things he shouldn't, and so am I. I'm finished with this. We all know better, and if we keep it up, we're going to disappoint Mom."

They got angry with me because I always found out what they were doing. Both of them loved and respected our mother though, and they agreed to stop skipping school.

There were other things that put a strain on our relationship, such as the way David behaved when we had to do chores together. It was our responsibility to wash and dry the dishes after dinner. He constantly did things to irritate me such as playing "gotcha last" or snapping a towel at my arms and legs. He didn't think he should have to help with kitchen duty since he had a paper route, and it was his responsibility to either mow the lawn or shovel snow depending on the season. To spare myself from being annoyed and to get the job done more quickly, I'd enlist Rick to help instead. We worked well together because he didn't want to be stuck in the kitchen any longer than I did. Rick knew that if we didn't do a good job, we'd be called back to wash everything again. The other benefit of having him help me was that I had a chance to talk to him about some of the things David was doing. I tried to help him understand that talking back to our dad would only make things worse. As much as I hated school, I knew it wasn't a good idea to skip classes and tried to convince Rick likewise.

David had as much reason to hate our father as I did. I had watched countless times as my father would beat him for the slightest offense. An untimely glance or a misinterpreted word was enough to trigger a violent response. My father was always eager to show that he was the boss, and much stronger than David. Rick and I would beg our dad to stop, but most often he just turned on us. "Do you want some of the same?!" he'd bark.

Knowing that we shared in our daily torment, David would come to me in hopes that I would validate his misbehavior. As often as he could, he tried to make life difficult for our father. Sometimes it was an act as simple as hiding one of my father's books where he couldn't find it. He was frequently sarcastic, and constantly mouthed-off to my dad. David also neglected his chores, occasionally as part of a far-fetched idea. David would avoid mowing the lawn in an attempt to pass the responsibility back to my dad, who suffered from hay fever and asthma. He anticipated that yard work would cause Dad to have an asthmatic attack and maybe – just maybe – it would kill him. Of course that plan never even got past the first stage. My father wasn't about to let David sidestep his chores. He just brought more punishment on himself. I hated to watch the beatings as much as I hated receiving them. When David was being punished, I knew it could spill over to me at any second. All it took was for my crying to catch my father's attention, and then he'd snarl, "What are you crying for? Do you want to be next?" I tried over and over to explain to my brother that his insubordination was more trouble than it was worth, but he insisted on his own way. His desire to create conflict always puzzled me. I felt it was in my best interest to do whatever I could to keep the peace. Whether that meant doing extra work around the house or faking laughter at my father's jokes, it was an insignificant price to pay for improving his mood and getting on his good side.

David and I would get into trouble if we were caught whispering, so we went for walks to vent our frustration and anger. Sometimes we walked for two hours or longer. There was no denying that we both hated our father and even wished he would soon meet a violent end, but while David's every thought seemed to revolve around vengeance, my focus was on self-preservation. I tried to remind him what the Bible says about revenge.

Rom 12:17	Repay no one evil for evil. Have regard for good things in the sight of all men.
Rom 12:18	If it is possible, as much as depends on you, live peaceably with all men.
Rom 12:19	Beloved, do not avenge yourselves, but *rather* give place to wrath; for it is written, *"Vengeance is Mine, I will repay,"* says the Lord.
Rom 12:20	Therefore *"If your enemy is hungry, feed*

> him; If he is thirsty, give him a drink; For in so doing you will heap coals of fire on his head."

Rom 12:21   Do not be overcome by evil, but overcome evil with good.

He usually just scoffed at my attempts to apply what we had learned in Sunday school. He dismissed my advice, saying "It never gets better anyway. I don't care. I'll get him back somehow."

"Do you think I like the way he treats us? Do I have to remind you that he beat me until I went into shock because I couldn't learn my spelling list for school?" My father had made me stand in front of him, spelling each word after he read it from the list. If I missed a letter, he struck the back of my bare legs with the yardstick until I got it right. He continued the torture word after word until finally my body and mind couldn't take any more and I fell to the floor in shock. "Don't you remember how terrified he was, and how he had to use first aid to bring me around? Do you remember the black and blue marks, and how I had to wear long stockings to cover them? I hate him very much, and I wish he would die! But I still think if we pray God will help!"

Either he couldn't or didn't want to believe me, but I still tried to convince him. "I know he's not going to change, and things aren't going to get any better as long as we live with him, but some day we will be old enough and we'll be able to leave. Someday I'll meet someone who would love me for the person I am. We will never treat our children the way he treats us. We'll love our children and we'll be an example of the right way to raise a family for the Lord."

Our younger brother, Rick, was with us when we had these conversations. He was too young to understand what we were talking about. As he grew older, he also became a target of Dad's aggression, although not to the extent to which David and I experienced it. We each had our own particular battle with him. No one escaped unharmed.

It was a terrible feeling to be afraid of looking my own father in the eye. Whenever I walked through the house it felt as if I were back in the woods at Houghton Lake, trying to slip away without being noticed by the bear. He was an unpredictable beast. If I got too close, he would pull me down onto his lap and start groping me or reach under my skirt and pull my underwear down. It didn't mater if the boys, Mom, or Granddad were in the room. He didn't care as long as he got his way. Sometimes when he caught me off guard I would end up falling to the floor. He'd then take the opportunity to pull my underwear off, throw them at me and laugh. Humiliation and impotent rage overwhelmed me.

I didn't want to feel helpless anymore. I had to do something to stop him from ever hurting us again. One day when only my grandfather and I were home, I took my brother's baseball bat and put it at the end of my bed. If my dad started another fight with David, I'd be ready to bash in his skull. I didn't have to wait long for him to present me with an opportunity. I can't even remember exactly what David had said or done to set him off that evening, but my dad's anger erupted once again. It started in the kitchen and as usual, and David tried to get away by simply leaving the room. As he stepped into the dining room, dad was close behind, breathing down his neck causing David to quicken his pace. He made it as far as my room (the sitting room) and down he went right in front of me, pushed to the floor by my father. As he scrambled to get up, dad grabbed David's right foot and began twisting it. I jumped onto the sofa and watched in horror as Dad straddled David, grabbed and squeezed his throat, and began to pound his head against the floor. My mind raced. "What should I do?! What should I do?!"

I wanted so badly to reach for the baseball bat next to the sofa and take a swing at my father's head, but I couldn't bring myself to do it. I was paralyzed with the fear that I'd miss my father and hit David instead. My heart was pounding so hard I could almost hear it. My father held on tight, and David's face turned red. "God, oh God! Please help!"

Mom rushed in and yelled, "Stephen! Stephen! Stop it! You're going to kill him!"

"I *am* going to kill him! He can't talk to me that way!"

Fortunately, though, my father released his hold. He rose to his feet and looked down at David. As my brother gasped for air and struggled to stand, my dad said, "That will teach you to keep your mouth shut. Don't you ever talk to me that way again."

Mom helped David up, and told him to go to his room

and stay for a while. He did exactly that, and my dad went back into the kitchen, still yelling at my mom to stop interfering with his discipline. I thought, "So even if you kill someone for the sake of discipline, it's ok? Why couldn't I use the bat on him? I guess that would make me just as bad as he is."

Then I thanked God for stopping me from doing something I would undoubtedly regret. "I know that the Bible says 'Vengeance is mine, says the Lord. I will repay'. I can't do anything about it, so please...just don't let my dad kill David."

However, the struggle with thoughts of killing my father continued. I found myself dwelling on how much I hated him, and I immersed myself in fantasies of revenge. Another idea that seemed realistic enough to try began with sneaking into the kitchen for a butcher knife. During the day when no one was nearby, I tiptoed to the counter and opened the drawer. As quietly as I could, I rummaged through the utensils until I found a knife that was large enough to be deadly, but small enough to hide. I shook with fear of being caught as I went to the sofa where I slept and placed the knife under it in a spot where I could reach it when I went to bed. My plan was to lay it on my stomach under the covers and wait for my dad to come over to me. If he began to lie on top of me, I would raise the blade of the knife for him to impale himself right through his big fat belly.

While I lay in bed waiting, I started to consider what I was about to do. I wondered what would happen if something were to go wrong with my plan. On the other hand, what if it worked? What if I really did kill my father? Could I live with what I had done? Would I go to reform school or even prison? There was no more peace to be found in murdering my dad than there was in living with him. If I believe God sees everything my father is doing, then he must also see everything that I do. I remembered the sixth commandment, and put my plan on hold indefinitely. I put the knife back under the cot until I had a chance to sneak it back into the kitchen.

Even when a perfect opportunity presented itself, I couldn't take it. During our annual summer vacation when I was sixteen, things were going pretty much the same way they always did. My dad spent his time on the lake fishing, my mom was relaxed at the cabin, and my brothers and I explored the park. During this particular summer, I was offered work at the nearby restaurant. One afternoon I was headed back to the cabin to get ready for my shift, and I saw Dad approaching in the boat. I went down to the dock to help bring his things to the house, and mom met us moments later. The two of us grabbed an armload of supplies and took them to our cabin. Mom stayed back to put them away, and I walked back to get another load. As I scooted down the little hill that sloped down to the shore, I saw Dad unhook the motor while still standing in his aluminum boat. I arrived at the dock and watched as he straightened up and balanced the motor on the edge of the boat. The weight, however, proved to be too much and tipped the boat, ejecting my father into the water with the motor falling in on top of him. I stood on the edge of the dock looking down at him, trapped under water with the motor resting comfortably on his chest while he struggled to free himself. I couldn't believe my response when I had time to consider it later. All I could do was laugh uncontrollably. It wasn't until my mom came back to the dock that I regained my composure. She asked where my father was and, still laughing, I pointed down at him. Hardly amused, she yelled "Janeen! Do something before he drowns!"

Mom couldn't swim, so it was up to me to help him. The water wasn't very deep, so I was able to quickly jump in and push the motor off of him. He jumped up through the surface of the water and when he caught his breath, the first words out of his mouth were, "You idiot! You are so stupid! What were you thinking? You think that's funny?!"

"No, I really don't. I'm sorry."

That wasn't exactly true. It was a great feeling to see him so vulnerable. For those few moments while he was trapped underwater, I had the power to save him or let him drown. It gave me a feeling of victory over him, even if it was short lived. After that incident, I stayed away from him. I figured it was best to stay out of sight until he cooled off.

Many times when I read my Bible, I felt conviction over the hatred I felt for my father. I was truly sorry about my death wish for him, but I really needed to feel loved by someone. I remember quietly crying out to the Lord, asking

Him to let me feel comforted as if I were curled up in His lap. I thanked him for being there and for listening to me. One verse I had memorized was in Psalms:

Psa 19:14   Let the words of my mouth and the meditation of my heart be acceptable in Your sight, O LORD, my strength and my Redeemer.

Sometimes my brother's solution seemed much more appealing. My parents kept a bowl on the top of the buffet in our dining room as a place to deposit pennies all year so we could afford a turkey at Thanksgiving. I began to steal one penny at a time until I had pilfered enough of them to buy a bottle of aspirin. The next time I was sent to buy groceries, I took the pennies with me and purchased the aspirin separately from the items on the list my mother gave me. "Now I have the answer", I thought. "Tonight it will be over."

I was so happy that I could hardly wait to take the pills. After everyone was in bed, I quietly went into the closet to retrieve the bottle from my coat pocket, then to the kitchen for a glass of water. One after another, I swallowed the pills until the bottle was empty. There were forty-eight of them. After I finished, I went back to bed believing I would never wake up. Morning came, and the usual sounds of my parents and brothers getting ready to start another day roused me from my sleep. I began to mentally prepare for the daily routine when I remembered what I had done. Quickly taking stock of any pains or other symptoms that might result from an overdose, I realized I had none. I had slept through the entire night and awoke in the morning without as much as a stomach ache.

A more creative, though less efficient idea stemmed from my interest in sewing. I had grown up watching my mother do embroidery work and my grandmother sew dresses for my doll. I had tried to sew when I was younger, but I seemed to be all thumbs. After my grandmother died, I became interested again and gave it another shot. The practice I got from making and selling pot holders and stuffed elephants gave me confidence that I could do well in the high school sewing class. The only problem was having enough money to buy the materials for the dress each of us made as a final project. Thankfully, the Lord took care of that by providing a job for me at a card shop not far from home. I loved learning to sew, and I had a great teacher I got along with very well. But even during those enjoyable hours, my mind was never fully distracted from the struggle I would face yet again once I went home. I was unable to just enjoy placing the next pin in the right place or making that next stitch.

One day while I was working on the dress, an idea (one that was not very well thought out) came to me. "What if I begin swallowing the straight pins?"

I imagined that if I could get one or two of them down, they would put a hole somewhere in my stomach or my intestines. Then hopefully an infection would form and sicken me. If I could delay a visit to the hospital long enough, maybe it would kill me. At first I just put the pins in my mouth while I worked. It was a fairly natural thing to do while sewing, since I didn't have a free hand to hold the pin.

I thought that if I kept one in my mouth long enough, I would either forget that it was there or become distracted and "accidentally" swallow it. Intending to avoid that very situation, our teacher threatened to mark down anyone caught with pins in their mouth. Now it seems strange to think that I didn't care whether I lived or died, but I didn't want to take the risk of getting a low grade in my sewing class. It didn't stop me from trying once I got home. Walking around the house with pins in my mouth didn't seem to make much sense, so I took a more direct approach. I put one in my mouth, dull end first, and swallowed. I figured that if I swallowed them point-first, they would just get stuck in my throat and would cause an injury that would probably not be life threatening, and might only serve to draw attention to my suicide attempt. Even if they did stick in my throat, the thought of dying from an infection seemed more tolerable than the possibility of choking to death. I found out that they went down rather easily, so I swallowed another one. I waited a few days and nothing happened, so I ate a couple more. They passed right through me and I never felt even a hint of discomfort.

It made me angry that I had tried so hard to kill myself and I couldn't even do that right. Maybe Dad was right when he said I was only good for keeping bread from going moldy.

"Why don't you want me, God? What are you trying to teach me? I do love You, so if I can't die, then at least take care of me and let me show how a Christian family should be raised. Help me to be a good mother who will do whatever it takes to protect my children."

Chapter 9

Continuous Violations

When I was fourteen, an evangelist came to our church to hold meetings for two weeks. He was a powerful speaker, and always inspired the congregation to have a great desire to pray. The church was opened early each night so that people could pray before the service started. Our family was always among the first to arrive, and the last to leave. During those meetings I pleaded with God for changes in my life and my father's life. I wanted so badly to love my dad and for him to just be a good father. I told the Lord that no matter what happened in my life, I wanted to serve Him. I began to read my Bible more and pray differently. Instead of dwelling only on my desire for security, I first praised and thanked God for the things I knew by faith that he would do for me. Next I asked for better health and for God to give me a real love for my dad. I prayed for my grandfather to carefully consider his words before he spoke, rather than always saying the first thing that came to his mind. Last, I prayed for the Lord to either stop my father from abusing us or to take me to Heaven. I remember so well seeing my dad kneel in prayer, and hoping that things would change. But I knew him all too well. He would leave me alone for a while, and then go back to his old ways. He even claimed that the Lord had really worked in his life and that he was a different person, but his words didn't mean much. I had about three weeks of peace before he slipped back into the same pattern of behavior.

    One Wednesday evening, my dad had decided he was tired and would stay home from church. While my mom got ready for church, he took a nap. The boys were out with their friends who lived nearby, and Grandpa was sitting in his green velvet chair in the living room just beyond my parents' bedroom. Mom had reminded me that once my homework was finished I was supposed to do some of the ironing. She left to catch the bus, and I continued washing the dishes. After a few minutes, I finished up and went on to my homework. I didn't have much assigned to me that day, so I was looking forward to having some free time after I ironed. I was planning on washing and setting my hair before I went to bed. Doing my hair gave me a sense of pride. I had mastered a hairstyle called the bustle-back, which was considered very fashionable at the time. I completed the last of my homework and began to iron. The house was still very quiet. About ten minutes passed and I heard steps coming my way from the dining room. I recognized the sound of my father's heavy footfall, and I began to tense up with fear. I kept my eyes on my work, thinking that he might just pass by if I didn't make eye contact.

    What I heard next was the very thing I dreaded. "Psst...psst...Sis, come take a nap with me."

    He knew that my mother wouldn't be home for at least three hours, and the boys would be gone for almost as long so he was free to do what he wanted. I told him that I needed to finish the ironing. That only made him more determined to get his way. He came over to where I was working, stepped past the ironing board, and then bent down and yanked the power cord out of the socket. He told me to put the iron down. Oh, how tempted I was to pick it up and slam it into his face. Fearing the consequences of a successful or failed attempt forced me to obey him. I set the iron down on the board, and he grabbed me by the ear and pulled me into his room. "Now lay down", he said.

Once I was in bed, he lied down next to me and draped his heavy arm over me. "Now isn't that better than standing in the living room ironing?"

It took all of the nerve I could muster to say, "Well, I'm not really tired. I need to get my ironing finished, and you know I don't like doing this."

"Finish it some other time. Just lay here and get cozy with me for a while."

I lay on my back frantically praying and asking God for help. I thought that if I pretended to be asleep, my dad would leave me alone and go to sleep too. Then I would be able to slip away. It had actually worked a few times before, but it wasn't going to happen this time. He did think I had fallen asleep, but his hand started wandering anyway. Knowing that he was just getting started, I turned away from him to lie on my side. Then he knew I was awake, and he told me to stand up. I thought he was going to let me go, so I slid off the bed and started for the door. He caught me by the arm and said

"Just where do you think you're going? I didn't say you could leave."

As I stood before him, he began to tell me that I should never let boys touch me. He lifted my skirt and my slip, then pulled my underwear down and began to demonstrate just exactly what it was that he meant. I begged him to stop, but he wouldn't listen. He told me that I needed to know what boys were like and what they were after. Still unsatisfied, he said "Now I'll show you."

He opened his trousers and exposed himself, telling me to grab him. When I refused, he tried to force my hand. With tears running down my face, I resisted and hoped that one of the boys would come home and interrupt this nightmare. I wondered what my grandpa was thinking. Did he ever wonder why his son took me into the bedroom? Not that it mattered. He was too old and too frail to stand up to my father.

My dad forced me back to the bed, but I turned my back to him hoping he would go no further. "Dad, please let me go get the ironing done. I need to go. Please!"

"You just lay here and pretend you're my girlfriend."

He continued to grope me, and told me I "wasn't big enough yet". I finally broke away from him and ran out of the room. The condition he put himself in prevented him from chasing after me.

The next day, mom and I walked to the store and I got up the nerve to tell her what was going on when she went to church by herself. She had even seen some of the things I was telling her about, because my father was bold enough to do it right in front of her and my brothers. There was hell to pay if anyone interfered. Telling her about the abuse was hard enough, but it was even harder to hear her reply.

"Janeen, I don't have an answer for you. I have tried to talk to him about leaving you alone, but it only made things worse."

I had heard her confront him from time to time, saying "Stephen, stop it! Leave her alone. That isn't right."

His reply was always the same: "Mind your own business or you'll be sorry!"

If she continued to protest, it would set him off on a tirade that all the neighbors could hear. Then my father would blame me. "This is your fault! You know that, don't you?!"

Patricia had the misfortune of witnessing my father's brutality first hand. One Saturday, she came to my house and we sat and talked in the living room. I sat in my grandfather's chair. It was upholstered with striped green fabric, and had wood trim that decorated the top of the armrests and backrest. My father walked into the room and stopped in front of me. He asked me a question that I can no longer remember, but I know that I replied without sarcasm or belligerence. Nevertheless, he did not like my answer or, perhaps, the way that I answered so without warning he drew his arm back, and then brought his open hand across my face so fast and hard that my head slammed against the wood on the chair. I almost blacked out from the force of the blow. Patricia sat frozen with disbelief, and when I finally came to my senses I saw her staring at me, wide-eyed and terrified. I know that during times when the weather was warm and our windows were open, she had heard my father screaming at us and our frightened, broken voices crying for forgiveness and mercy. But this was the first time she had seen a demonstration of my father's temper with her own eyes. She continued staring in disbelief until she composed herself enough to say "I'll see you later" before hurrying out the door.

 I stayed in the chair, too stunned to do anything but sit and wonder what happened. I never got an explanation. Next I began to wonder if I would lose my best friend after what she had just seen. I worried that she may be too afraid to ever come back to my house again. I didn't want to think about it, so I just got up and tried to find something else to do. I tried to keep my mind occupied, but all I could think of was going over to my friend's house to see if she would still be my friend.

 I waited a couple of hours, and decided it was time to go next door. Waiting for someone to answer the door after I rang the bell was nerve wracking. I was just about to ring the bell a second time when one of Patricia's younger sisters opened the door. She knew why I was there and called for her big sister. Patricia came right away, and her first words were a relief to me. "Oh Ada, I am so sorry for you. I couldn't believe what your dad did!"

 She had told her mother what had happened, so now that the secret was out, I was free to speak about my father. Patricia's mother told me that she had often heard the shouting from our house as she sat crocheting at her dining room table. She told me how sorry she felt for all of us, and just knowing that someone else was aware of what was happening was very comforting. The secret was out again, and this time there was someone close to home I could turn to.

    I continued to read my Bible almost every night for the solace I so desperately needed. Time and time again I turned to Psalms to read King David's plea to God for deliverance and justice.

Chapter 10

Improvements and Relief

It wasn't until I was seventeen years old that I finally got a real bed. One day as my mom was on her way to the grocery store, she ran into a friend who lived in the neighborhood. Her daughter had just gotten married and left behind a single bed. The woman had no use for the extra bed and wanted to use the spare room for sewing, so she offered the bed to my mother for twenty five dollars. Finally, one of my prayers was being answered!

We pulled the bed home on the same wagon we used to haul wood for the furnace. Not only was I getting a good bed to sleep on, but I was also getting a blanket to keep me warm. No more would I have to get up in the middle of the night and go to the front hall closet for a winter coat to use as a blanket. I could hardly wait to lie down on my new mattress. That first night I went to bed early just because I wanted to be in a real bed. Lying there, all I could think was "Thank you, Father. Thank you for my bed!"

I didn't even want to go to sleep. I just wanted to enjoy the wonderful feeling of a soft mattress and the ability to turn from side to side without falling onto the floor. I even had a blanket that covered me completely! Praises to God were on my lips until I fell asleep. I couldn't believe the wonderful way he had answered my prayer after all those years. For quite a while after my new bed was brought into the house, the sight of it surprised me each time I walked through the house and saw it in the sitting room. I guessed that the Lord does grant our requests, but not always according to our schedule.

A short time later, my dad started pressuring my brother to find a girlfriend. David had been dating a girl during his senior year, but the relationship didn't work out so our father began to make suggestions about whom he should date.

A girl named Ruth started attending our church with her family. She was fifteen years old, and had a thirteen year old sister named Wanda and a twenty-six year old sister named Rebecca who had a child of her own. Rebecca was separated from her abusive husband, so they were all living together. Just about everyone at church knew about the violence Rebecca was trying to escape, and some feared that her husband may even hunt her down during a service. Not more than a month after she first came to our church, Rebecca's husband drove alongside her as she walked down the street, pointed a shotgun through the car's window, and shot her to death in front of her sisters. Her father suffered a major heart attack and died a short time later.

Ruth and Wanda's mother did her best to pull the family together and begin the healing process. Many people from our church donated their time, money, and much needed prayer. Our family was among several who took meals to their house from time to time. I became well acquainted with

Ruth and Wanda, and my parents got to know their mother. David was introduced to them at church, and after much teasing, pushing, and prodding from my Dad, he gave in and asked Ruth out on a date. Being only fifteen, she wasn't allowed to go out without taking her younger sister along. Many of their "dates" were spent simply playing games with either her family or ours. I often rode with David to Ruth's house, which was about twenty miles away. Even with someone special in his life, his behavior was very unpredictable. Sometimes we would have a good conversation; other times David would risk both our lives by racing across some railroad tracks to beat an approaching train or playing chicken with an oncoming car. I always had to carefully weigh my options when he asked if I would go with him.

On occasion his impulsive nature had humorous consequences. One Saturday evening, he stood on his girlfriend's front porch saying goodbye when he thought he spotted a black cat on the front lawn. He wasn't a fan of cats, so he whistled shrilly and clapped his hands to scare it away. He was annoyed when it paid no attention to him, so he leaped from the porch to chase it. Ruth and her mother yelled warnings to him, but he was too focused to hear them or notice the white stripe on the animal's back until it was too late. David tried to turn and get away from it, but he couldn't outrun the skunk's spray. When we returned home, he thought he could just quickly change into his pajamas and take his smelly clothes onto the back porch to air out. But as soon as we walked through the front door, the odor spread through the entire house. The smell was so strong that it woke my parents and Rick. My mom sent him back to the porch, and then she brought him a towel and made him strip outside. She then let him in and told him to go straight to the bathtub. Even with all the windows open and the fans turned on the smell was so strong that none of us were able to sleep well.

The next morning after breakfast, it was my turn to use the bathroom to get ready for church. All of my belongings were in that room, since there was no space for my dresser anywhere else. I always kept my necklace, wristwatch, Bible, and a few other personal items on top of it. I scanned the dresser's surface where everything was visible except for my watch. Taking a second glance, I realized it was hiding under a handkerchief that either my dad or one of my brothers had laid there. I put on the watch and I was ready to go. My parents, Rick, and I got into the family car, and David drove separately. A few minutes into the drive, mom said, "I still smell that skunk!"

We all agreed that we smelled it too, but we couldn't figure out where it was coming from. About the time we were pulling into the church parking lot, we realized that I was the one wearing the scent. The handkerchief that had been lying on top of my watch belonged to David, and the odor rubbed off on my fingers. All I could think of was spending the next three hours surrounded by people who were trying to identify the source of the awful smell. I decided to take preemptive action and tell my friends what had happened the night before. We all got a laugh out of it, which took the edge off my embarrassment.

David and Ruth continued dating, and their relationship grew more serious. One day after David had been dealt another unmerciful punishment, he came to me and told me that he was going to ask Ruth to marry him. I knew that in large part marriage was an escape route for him. I asked him where they would live and how he planned to provide for both of them, but he didn't have any solid answers. Ruth was still so young that her mother would need to sign consent forms to allow the marriage. She wanted them to wait, but she liked David very much and was glad to have a man in the house again. She wanted David and Ruth to live with her, but that was out of the question as far as he was concerned. He felt that she had already been too controlling while he was dating Ruth.

Our mom was disappointed because she wanted David to have a better job and a decent home before getting married. She also felt that neither one of them was emotionally prepared for the commitment, since they had both come from such tumultuous home lives.

Regardless of the diplomatic protests from both families, David had proposed, Ruth had accepted, and their decision was final. The word went out that they were going to be married and needed a place to live. A couple from church offered to rent them their basement apartment. It was very clean, fully furnished, and affordable which made it a perfect fit. The wedding took place three days before the Christmas of 1956. It was very small; just the two families followed by a quiet but enjoyable reception. Afterward, David and his new bride changed their clothes and were off to northern Michigan for their honeymoon and were home in time for the holiday.

With David married, my parents decided to let me move into the bedroom. Having an actual bedroom to sleep in was another wonderful answer to prayer. Rick and I always got along, so neither one of us minded sharing. David's old bed was given away, and we replaced it with mine. Rick helped me reassemble it, and he never complained once about having to share the room with me.

Unfortunately, with David gone I lost my ride to the Friday evening youth service at church. I had to start taking two busses to get there, and sometimes I wasn't allowed to go. Our neighborhood was becoming increasingly unsafe, and it was a good excuse for my father to keep me under his thumb. He was unhappy about me being involved in the choir and going to church activities. He said that it was unsafe for a young woman to be standing on the corner waiting for a bus in the dark, and would remind me about a young mother who had been murdered about a block away.

One Friday evening I had a close call of my own. I was riding the bus alone until the driver reached a stop where two men boarded. They noticed me right away, and it seemed like they had found just what they were looking for. Without saying a word to each other or me, one sat in front of me and the other across from me. They kept eyeballing me, and I knew I could be in for serious trouble. I glanced up at the bus driver, and I could see his eyes focused on us in his rearview mirror. Knowing that he was aware of the situation gave me a sense of relief. I still had a dilemma, though. What do I do when we come to my stop? I still had to catch another bus to take me the rest of the way to church, and I was sure they'd just get off the bus with me. I just kept looking out the window and prayed that God would help me know what to do. The only thing I could think of was to stay on the bus until the men got off, and then make my way back to my normal route. Unfortunately that could have meant missing church altogether.

Every couple of minutes I took another look around to reassess my situation. Each time I found the men still watching me and by this time they had begun making obscene gestures. Even more afraid, I watched the bus driver more closely, hoping he would not be too apathetic or intimidated to help. With one glance, or eyes met and he motioned for me to come to the front of the bus. I stood up and left my seat as quickly as I could, not giving the stalkers any time to react. We were not near a bus stop, so they had been expecting me to stay put for a while. I sat down right behind the driver, and he told me how he would help.

He turned his head to the left and leaned back to speak into my ear as I leaned forward. "I'm going to go past your usual stop, and cross the street so you'll have a shorter walk to your next pickup. I'll try to cross on the amber, so you'll have a green light to cross the street when I let you off. I'm going to stop suddenly and only open the door for a few seconds. Be ready to get off so I can shut the door behind you. Your bus is due in a couple of minutes, so they shouldn't be able to make it back in time to bother you. If you see them coming, just start yelling for help."

I said another prayer that everything would work out the way the driver had planned, and then began preparing myself to dash for the door. One of the men kept staring at me, and I just hoped that I could move faster than him. Giving no indication of what I was about to do, the driver and I kept talking and even laughing as we approached my stop. Then it was time. He drove through one last intersection, hit the brakes, and threw the lever to open the doors. I bolted from my seat and out onto the sidewalk. Just as he had planned, I had a green light and was able to run around the front of the bus and cross the street right away. By the time I set foot on the opposite side, the bus was driving away and I could see one of the men still peering through the window at me. I never told my parents about that incident. If I had, it would have virtually ended my social life with friends from church.

Even though the danger was very real, he never expressed concern for my mother's safety when she went to church alone on Wednesday nights. He knew that I was growing up and he was losing his control over me. I'm sure it also scared him that my friends in the choir would find out about him. As a deacon and a Sunday school teacher, he had a reputation to uphold. Still, he seemed to feel guilty for not giving me a ride. On some of the nights I had ridden the bus to the service or choir practice, I would find him waiting with my mom in the church parking lot to drive me home. Every once in a while we would stop for ice cream on the way. Sometimes I was glad for the ride and the ice cream, but sometimes I felt like I would choke on it. He made a habit of grilling me about the preacher's message and sharing his opinion. I had no desire to hear what he had to say about God or the Bible.

Nevertheless, I was glad to have a ride waiting for me in the winter. It was no fun to wait for the bus in cold weather. It reminded me of being very young, when my parents were unable to afford a car. But if I had to be cold and wet from time to time, at least it was because I was spending time with my friends and away from my dad.

As spring was right around the corner, I began looking forward to my senior year of high school. Knowing that I would be entering the twelfth grade was exciting, even though my health was still causing me to miss school often. My stomach problems kept me in the bathroom and made me late for class. It was nearly impossible to tell which foods were safe for me to eat, and which were making the problem worse. It seemed that there was no vegetable that agreed with me, but I couldn't rule out meat as the culprit, either. My doctor was unable to pinpoint the problem. My condition was worsening each day. I was in constant pain, and couldn't maintain a healthy weight.

One day as I sat in class, I became very ill and knew I wasn't going to be able to stay for the rest of my classes. My teacher was very perceptive and understanding. She could see that something was very wrong with me, and she told me that if I needed to use the restroom I could go at any time and wouldn't need a pass. In my next class the teacher wasn't as kind. She wouldn't give me a hall pass, so I left without her permission. When I tried to return, she sent me to the counselor's office. The counselor told me that I would not be allowed back into the classroom that day, nor would I be excused to use the restroom anymore. He also refused my request to use the telephone so I could have my mother pick me up. Fortunately, one of my friends worked as an office assistant, and once the counselor left his office she let me make the call. Hearing my mom pick up the phone was like a breath of fresh air. I told her what had happened, and she was very upset by the way I had been treated. She told me she would call a taxi right away, and I should watch for it to pull up in front of the school. I thanked my friend and hurried back to the chair that faced the counselor's desk and sat down in case he came back before the taxi arrived.

I was relieved to know that I would be at home soon, and relieved to know that my mother had really listened to me and had sympathy. I knew that something significant had to be done about my health, and hoped that she would agree.

The taxi arrived after just a few minutes, and I was home just a few more minutes after that. Once I entered the house, my mom told me that she had already called the doctor, who said that I needed to be in the hospital. I couldn't believe what I was hearing; finally I was going to get some help!

After dinner that evening, my dad drove me to the hospital. With each mile that passed, the joy of knowing that another prayer was being answered filled my heart. Not only would I get some relief from my stomach aches, but I would also get time away from my dad. I thanked God over and over again.

Once we reached the hospital, I found the staff to be extremely caring. I was checked in, and after arriving at my room the nurse asked my parents not to stay much longer because a complete physical would need to be performed. Hearing that scared me a little, but I figured it couldn't be much worse than what I was going through at home.

I spent the next three weeks in the hospital undergoing a battery of tests, as well as experiments with my diet. My stay there was as pleasant as it could have been. I shared a large room with four other ladies who treated me as if I were an old friend. The hospital staff was also very kind and caring.

After a series of x-rays and blood tests, my doctors discovered that I had a condition called colitis, and that I was hypoglycemic. I had several conversations with dieticians, who helped me understand how my diet would have to change. I was very disappointed to find out that fruits and vegetables had been the major source of my stomach problems, but I was ready to do whatever was necessary to have some relief. I was also prescribed some medicine for my stomach, and a strong tranquilizer. Earlier, the doctor had asked me if anything was troubling me at home, because my diet was only half of the reason for my symptoms. Stress and anxiety accounted for the other half. I couldn't bring myself to tell him the truth about my father, but I'm sure he sensed that I was hiding something. He gave me a self-help book called "How to Live 365 Days a Year". He told me that in order to reduce the amount of stress in my life, I would either need to quit the job I had at the local card shop or drop out of school. I desperately wanted to graduate from high school, so the choice was clear.

After the doctor left, the ladies in my room said that I should have told him about my father. I hadn't even said much to them. I was too ashamed to mention the sexual abuse, so I had only told them that my dad was very mean. I thought more about their advice and everything the doctor had told me, and decided to call my mother. I hoped she would be willing and able to reason with my dad, but I could never be sure how she'd respond.

I dialed the phone and after a couple of rings, my mother answered. She seemed pleasantly surprised to hear my voice and asked if I had seen the doctors again.

"Yes", I said. "The tests are all finished, and now I'm on a diet and have to take some pills to help my stomach. But that's not the reason for my call. The doctor wanted me to talk to you about things that are troubling me because they're part of the reason I'm sick."

"What do you mean?"

I quickly prayed, "Oh Lord, help me to say what I need to say."

I kept my explanation brief and frank. "I need him to stop putting his hands where they don't belong, and to stop pulling my underwear off. He has to stop forcing me to take naps with him. And he has to stop forcing his way into the bathroom when I'm using it!"

"Janeen, I will take this to the grave with me. I will not tell your father. I don't believe this!"

"Mom, you know it's true! You've seen for yourself what he does to me!"

"Well, you know when I was growing up, I had a problem with a man...but you just have to get over it."

"But this is my father", I protested. "He's doing it all the time, and that's what's causing my stomach pains. The doctor said much of my symptoms are caused by stress and anxiety!"

By this time, she just wanted to get off the phone. Before hanging up, she told me she didn't think they would be coming out to visit me that evening. That was ok with me; the medication I was on made me very drowsy and I just wanted to go to sleep anyway.

Apparently my mother accepted the truth in what I had said, and relayed the message to my dad. I knew she had told him as soon as the phone next to my bed began to ring. As apprehensive as I was about answering, I took comfort in the fact that my dad was a few miles away.

The first words from his mouth were, "Is that really the way you want it?!"

I was dumbfounded by such a ridiculous question, but said "yes".

"Fine! If that's the way you want it, you won't have to worry about talking to me anymore because I will never speak to you again as long as I live!" With that, he hung up on me.

He had missed the whole point...it was his hands that were the problem.

I had a feeling that his promise wouldn't last long, and I was right. My parents came to visit me the next evening, and every evening until I was discharged from the hospital. Thanks to the drugs I had been given, I slept through their first visit after the hostile phone call. The next evening they brought me a bag of Jewish pastries. I'd never had so much food available to me in all my life.

I was eventually taken off the tranquilizer and my appetite began to improve. The doctors checked my weight, and felt I was on the road to recovery. I met with the dietician again, who recapped the guidelines of my no sugar, high protein diet. Soon after that, I was released from the hospital.

To my surprise, my parents made sure I got the right food and enough of it. Neither of my parents earned much money, but my dad cut back on his weekly purchase of two pounds of Sander's candy so that we could buy some additional food. Fortunately, he had very good medical insurance through his job which covered almost all of the hospital bills. Even better, he seemed to be keeping his distance without giving me the silent treatment as he promised.

Chapter 11

Transformation

A few weeks later I had another opportunity to go to church camp. It was the last year I would be eligible to go. After the terrible school year and three week stay in the hospital caused by colitis I had been diagnosed with, I was really looking forward to a week away. I just wanted to be with my friends and forget about everything. I still hated my father and struggled with faith in God's presence in my life.

This year, a young, dynamic pastor from a small town in Michigan was the guest preacher. The topic of his sermons was forgiveness. It was the last thing I wanted to hear, so on the first night I snuck away from my church group and hid until chapel was over. I had to be careful when I rejoined them. If a counselor caught me, I would be sent home. If my friends saw me return, they'd know I skipped. It seems silly that sometimes our faith allows us to trust God for deliverance when we sin, but does not motivate us to make the right choice in the first place. I panicked and tried to bribe God, "Oh God, please get me out of this mess and I promise I will never do it again!"

The counselors didn't catch me, but my friends did. They asked me where I had been, and I lied. My conscience bothered me terribly, and I ended up telling them the truth. I felt so bad that I knew I'd have to go to chapel the next evening.

I sat at the back of the chapel and tried to tune out the preacher, but it didn't work. The harder I tried to ignore his message, the more of it I heard. It seemed that God was speaking only to me through the preacher, telling me that He loved me and cared about what happened to me. It gave me a minor sense of reassurance, and made me just a little bit more receptive to what he had to say. On the third night I sat with my friends, but still tried to ignore the preacher as he explained to us why we must forgive others whenever and however they hurt us. He quoted the books of Romans and Matthew:

Rom 5:8	But God demonstrates His own love toward us, in that while we were still sinners, Christ died for us.
Mat 6:14	"For if you forgive men their trespasses, your heavenly Father will also forgive you.
Mat 6:15	"But if you do not forgive men their trespasses, neither will your Father forgive your trespasses.

The entire sermon seemed to be tailor-made for me. The preacher said that we must let go of the hate we have. It is sin, and has no place in the life of a Christian. I needed so badly for my prayers to be answered, and I knew that my unrepentant attitude regarding my anger was a hindrance to my relationship with God. I couldn't get through the next few years of living at home without His help. I had to ask the Lord to transform me, and never let me have hatred in my heart for anyone ever again.

The altar call came, and I was prepared to kneel at the front of the chapel to pray. Usually a counselor would meet you and pray with you, but I prayed for the Lord to keep anyone from approaching me. I just wanted to be alone with Him. I made my way down the aisle, and made it to the front by myself. I fell to my knees, buried my head in my folded arms, and broke into tears. I told God how I feared and hated my dad, though he knew it already. I told him that I wanted to kill my dad or myself – either one was ok with me – but he knew that too. He had seen the baseball bat and the knife I had hidden under my bed, and He had seen me swallow the pills and the straight pins. I was a Christian, but I had let sin rule over me for too long. Now, just as I had done as a five year old child, I began crying out to God for forgiveness. I asked him to lift the burden of hatred I carried every day. I wanted to truly have the joy of my salvation, rather than simply project the image of a happy Christian to outsiders.

When I finished praying, I opened my eyes and stood up to see that I was the only one left in the chapel. I felt as though the weight of the world was lifted from my back. I returned to my cabin, and my friends immediately began asking me what had happened and where I'd been. They told me what time it was, and it wasn't until then that I realized I had been praying for four hours.

In the morning I still felt forgiven, and now felt very free to love my dad in a way that I had never known before. I knew that I didn't have that ability on my own. I wasn't even frightened by the thought of seeing my dad again, and the rest of the week was wonderful.

When the last evening at camp had come, I made my way to the main road to watch for my parents' car. I spotted it after a few minutes, and doubt already crept back into my mind. "Now we'll see how you really feel", I thought.

But as soon as the words entered my mind, the Lord reminded me of Joshua 1:5 - "I will never leave thee nor forsake thee". Times like those have proven to me the value of memorizing scripture.

Once the car was parked and everyone got out, I waked over and hugged my mom and Rick and greeted my dad with sincere friendliness. "Come on! I want to show you some of the things we've been doing and you can meet some of my friends."

There were no cross looks or gruff words. I couldn't believe how smoothly it went. "Thank you, Lord", I thought.

It was the beginning of a new life. I had become the happy person I always wanted to be, even though I knew I would have to go back into that same house. I would still have to trust Him to remove me from my father's reach, and to help me with my health. He had not yet changed my circumstances, but He had changed me.

Chapter 12

Life After High School

The beginning of my senior year drew near, as did my nineteenth birthday. I was going to be the oldest student in my graduating class. I had repeated the 3rd and 5th grades because of my poor health, so I was overjoyed to finally be close to graduating. After I was released from the hospital, my health had stabilized so I started singing in the choir again. God also blessed me by bringing several good friends into my life. The choir director, Richard, and his wife Joyce volunteered to drive me to practice and the young adults' service. That meant I no longer had to wait for two busses each time I needed to be at the church. I had also become close with two other women, Donna and Mary. All of them regularly told me that they were praying for me. They all knew about my struggle with colitis, but only Donna knew anything about my abusive father. I was careful not to tell her much, because our fathers had known each other since childhood and I was certain my dad would find out if I spoke out.

Things were looking up for me. I was sleeping better because I had my own room and my dad had been leaving me alone. My health was better, and school was going well. I had a sewing class that I really enjoyed. I had even won 1st place in a sewing contest which required me to make my own dress. My teacher was so impressed with it that she asked if she could put it on display in the hallway showcase for a few weeks. I was extremely honored to have my hard work recognized.

There were still challenges at school, mainly because of the violent kids there. I had seen a boy slammed against a locker, splitting his head open. Another student was killed at the football field during a game. I had even had a guy put a knife to my back and demand my lunch money. I lifted my lunch bag over my head so he could see that I wasn't buying food, and to draw attention to what was happening. It made him uncomfortable enough to say "I was just kidding" and leave. I didn't want to bring any more trouble on myself, so I didn't turn around to get a look at him. The teachers seemed powerless to do anything about the violence anyway. They were just as likely to be targets as students were. Much like my home life, I got through each day by keeping a low profile and avoiding conflict any way I could.

I hoped and prayed that I could stay healthy long enough to get a decent job after I finished school. That way I could get a place of my own and never have to deal with my dad again. A man from our church promised that there would be a job for me at the company he worked for once I graduated. Unfortunately, my sister-in-law had a more immediate need for work and she was already available, so she was given the job. I was very disappointed, but I was enjoying everything that came with being in the twelfth grade. There were pictures to be taken for the year book, senior skip day, and our class trip.

My friend Patricia went to an all-girls school, so she asked me if I could set her up with someone so we could go on double dates. Reminding her that I didn't have a boyfriend, and wasn't even allowed to date didn't deter her. She pleaded with me to ask my parents again if I could start dating, and I caved in. There was a boy named Bob who had been asking me out since the ninth grade, and was once again pursuing me. I liked him very much as a friend, but nothing more.

Much to my surprise, my parents gave me permission to go out with Bob for the events surrounding our graduation. Once I gave Bob the news, I asked him about his good friend Bryan. Bryan didn't have a date yet, so I gave his picture to Patricia and vice-versa. They both liked what they saw, so our plan for double dates was worked out well. Bob and I didn't continue dating after graduation, but Patricia and Bryan stayed together and married soon after finishing college.

With graduation over and no job in sight, I began to feel lost and wish I had not quit my job at the card shop. She was surprisingly upset with me when I told her I couldn't continue working, so I knew I wouldn't be welcome back. The U.S. economy was in a recession in 1957, so jobs were scarce. I kept praying about it without receiving an answer. I was in a holding pattern, and once again had to worry about my dad. Almost as soon as the doctors determined that I was healthy enough to stop taking some of the medication, he went back to his old ways.

Even though the Lord had removed the hate from my heart, I struggled to stay on the right path. With my dad constantly molesting me and no apparent way to make a living, I considered running away and entering a life of prostitution. I figured that if someone was going to use my body, at least I could be paid for it. I wasn't very confident about my chances at finding a husband anyway. If I did meet someone and fell in love, I'd have to tell him what I'd been through. Who would want me after hearing that? Even with all my negativity, Bible verses still crept to the front of my mind. I thought of Psalm 3:5-6:

Psa 3:5	I lay down and slept; I awoke, for the LORD sustained me.
Psa 3:6	I will not be afraid of ten thousands of people Who have set *themselves* against me all around.

That would have comforted me more if I had felt like God was directing my path. Where was the guy that would want me?

One day David called us to invite us over for dinner for the first time. They were still renting the basement apartment from our friends. When we arrived, we saw that we were not the only ones invited. David's in-laws were also there. As David and Ruthie served us dessert, David made an announcement. "I've got a surprise for everyone…we'll be having a baby in April!"

We all congratulated him and Ruthie, and they asked us to keep our eyes open for a new place to live.

I began to wonder if that might mean I would finally have a job. Ruthie did say that she hadn't been feeling well, and probably wouldn't be able to keep working. Having to ride the bus to work every day wasn't easy for her. That was all I needed to hear. I started planning a way to approach her boss to ask for the job if Ruthie resigned. I never got the chance though, since my mom beat me to it. She asked Bill the very next time she saw him at church. He told her that I was at the top of his list, but he wouldn't be hiring until September. That was fine with me! Just knowing that a job was in my future lifted my spirits and I started to believe that I would soon have a way out of my oppressive home life.

Long before I began working, I had big plans for how I would spend my money. First on my list was to buy some decent clothes for my new job. Before that time, I never had a reason or the money to buy clothing that was suitable for an office setting. Of course I would also need a clock radio so I would be sure to wake up on time. I had to remember to set aside ten percent for the offering at church, too. Finally, I would go to the dentist. I had only been to the school dentist twice, and had my front teeth fixed when they had been knocked out so I never had regular cleanings. I had to save whatever was left over. It was the only way I'd be able to move out. However, all these plans were on hold until I was actually offered the job. I continued waiting throughout the summer, thanking God for providing an answer to prayer. I still had to dodge my dad constantly, but one by one the obstacles that kept me from a normal life were being torn down.

In mid-September, the day finally came when I received a call from Bill, who asked me to come in for an interview. The date was set, and the ball was rolling. On my way to the interview, I was extremely nervous. The office was not far from Tiger Stadium, in a neighborhood that was worse than my own. Looking through the windows of the bus I saw houses with broken windows and wide-open doors. Children ran shoeless into the street, and I could see that their clothes were raggedy and their little hands and faces were filthy. But the location wasn't all that made me nervous. I knew that my resume was less than extraordinary. I had never worked in an office before…only a dime store, a card shop, and a restaurant. Now I would probably have to type and do who knows what else.

Bill came out to greet me, and then led me back to his office. He gave me the usual company policy documents to read, and once I finished he began telling me the job requirements. That was when I finally began to relax. It would be my job to file papers, answer phones, sort mail, and make trips to the post office in downtown Detroit or across the river in Windsor. The tasks were varied, and I knew I'd never be bored. The interview was mostly a formality, so I was offered the job right away. I started working the next day at a rate of $1.25/hour. I had and awesome feeling of self-worth to be a part of the work force.

It wasn't long before I figured out that $1.25 an hour wasn't going to get me out of my parents house anytime soon. As I had planned, the first thing I bought was new clothing. Mom and I went downtown after work, and I got everything I needed. I came home with one black jumper, a white blouse, gray shoes, a gray purse, two sweaters and a skirt. I still had money left over to put in the offering plate on Sunday, and some to save for long term goals. Then I went to the dentist. After poking and prodding for a while, he told me that I had twenty-two cavities that needed to be filled. I hadn't planned on such a large expense, but I was determined to have my teeth fixed. I also had to start paying forty dollars in room and board to my parents. After sitting down with paper and a pencil to make a budget, I was disappointed to find out how little cash I would be able to save each month. Once again I had to turn to God. "Lord, now what?! I really need help here."

From then on I used layaway plans for anything I wanted, starting with the clock radio. I found a little pink one I liked, and it was twenty-five dollars. I could hardly wait for the day I was allowed to pick it up. It was difficult to keep my mind on my work, and waiting for the bus seemed to take forever. Once I arrived at the store and made my last payment, I still had to wait for the sales clerk to retrieve the radio from the stockroom. Finally, it was mine and again I was thrilled at my ability to buy things for myself.

My mom was happy for me as well. I received a call from her at work one day, and she said "Janeen, I was just going down Fort Street and I saw a lovely pale green suit that

I think would look great on you. I thought you could put it in the layaway for Easter. It's at Winkelman's. Would you like me to meet you after work?"

She was right. It was a perfect fit, and I put it into layaway that evening. It was great to have Mom with me and see her happy for my success.

I was still hoping for the day I would meet someone special. There wasn't anyone I was interested in dating at that time, so I focused on doing what I could to improve my life. However, I continued to pray that God would send me a Christian husband. I asked for a man who would love me as a person, and not just for sex. I prayed that he would have the compassion and understanding to help me with emotional healing. He would also need to love our children. If we had a girl he must never have an impure thought toward her nor touch her inappropriately. I could picture my future husband and our life together clearly. He should be tall, with dark hair and dark eyes. He should have a college education and work in an office, so that he could take me to office parties. It really was a fantasy, but I knew that God can do anything and in John 16:24, the Bible says "…Ask, and you will receive, that your joy may be full."

One day after work, I came home to find that Grandpa was the only one home, and he wasn't in a very good mood. I quickly made my dinner and went into the living room to write a letter to my friend who was away at college. When I was about halfway done, the phone rang. I picked it up and was surprised to hear the voice of Jerry, a young man from church. After a couple minutes of small talk, he asked if I would like to go for a ride in his buddy's new Chevy. Without giving it much thought, I said "yes".

Once I hung up, I couldn't believe what I had done. How was I going to explain this to my dad? I knew Mom would be ok with it. "Maybe dad won't be too upset, since both of the boys were in his Sunday school class", I thought. "He's friends with Jerry's mother, too."

If Jerry's mother heard that I had gotten into trouble (at nearly twenty years old) for going on a date, she would almost certainly ask my dad why he was so strict. I convinced myself that he wouldn't make a big deal out of it, since it was so important to him to keep up the appearance of a loving Christian father.

I got ready, and tried to explain to Grandpa who I'd be with and where I'd be going. He seemed awfully confused, since I only went out on church activities, so I ended up leaving a note on the kitchen table. Then I said a quick prayer, asking God to allow me to have a good time without any punishment when I got home.

My friends arrived, and they made room for me in the car. We left the neighborhood, and got onto I-75. Then Jerry's friend decided to show off. A few seconds after merging, he hit the gas and we flew down the road at 100 miles per hour. I didn't have a romantic interest in Jerry to begin with, and now I was certain that these were not people I wanted to be spending much time with. I had come along for something to do and to be able to say that I had been on a date, but now I just wanted to get home safely. Thankfully, Jerry warned his friend that the car hadn't been broken in yet and he shouldn't be driving so fast. We slowed down, and made it to a restaurant safely. For the first time in my life, I actually had some optimism about the direction of my life. I had been through too much, and had come too far for it to end because of someone else's foolishness.

We finished dinner, and my friends returned me to my house without further incident. When I saw my parents I had to do some explaining, but it wasn't nearly as bad as it could have been. My dad did scold me even though he liked Jerry and often joked around with him at church. "Don't try that one again. If you want to go out with somebody, I need him to come to the house so I can talk with him. Don't be in such a hurry to get out of here! I don't care if you marry the garbage man, just as long as he is a Christian."

It made me very sad to know that my own father had such low expectations for me. . However, I knew the type of man I wanted and was willing to wait on God to send him.

****

I continued to work and save some money each month. I had a separate fund for a vacation I had been planning with my friend Mary since I started the job. She was ten years older than me, so my parents felt that I would be safe with her. We had narrowed our choices to either New York City or Washington D.C. and we decided to go during the week of Memorial Day, 1958. My dad said that New York was out, but D.C. would be alright with him.

Once again I had something to look forward to. The prospect of an upcoming vacation even made the dreary, cold days a bit more bearable. When I waited in the rain for a bus or trudged down the street in the snow, I would daydream about the day I would get to see the places I had only read about or seen on television. I was having some pain in my right side from time to time, but it was usually more of an annoyance than a major problem. There were days, however, when it would go on for hours with pains that would double me over. I just hoped it wouldn't ruin my trip.

The day came for our vacation, and our train was leaving after work. Mary's brother was going to drop her off at our house. I kept watching the clock, growing more certain with each passing minute that we'd miss our train. I prayed that my stomach would be ok at least until I got on the train. Mary arrived just in time for us to get to the train station. I couldn't help worrying about the car breaking down. "Why do I always have to think of so many things that would probably never happen" I wondered.

We loaded the suitcases into the car, and Mom, Dad, and Rick piled in with Mary and me. We quickly said goodbye and hurried onto the train. Mary and I were able to wave to my family once more as the train pulled away from the station. As it continued down the tracks, we went right past my street and the High School I had attended. I watched the pedestrians outside, knowing that they must be wondering where the train would take me, just as I had imagined where it would take the passengers I saw during my many walks along the tracks. It was a strange but wonderful feeling to have traded places with them.

I didn't get to have dinner the dining car (it was expensive and we needed to save money for the week ahead of us) but we were served a sandwich and a piece of fruit. As the evening progressed we traveled over beautiful landscapes, and stopped in little towns along the way to drop off and pick up passengers. The stops were just long enough to lock the sights into our memories. We continued further south and east, through the Appalachian Mountains. Neither Mary nor I had seen such beauty before that trip.

After dark I became aware of the pain returning to my side. It went on for hours, but I didn't tell my friend until it worsened. She asked if we should get off at the next stop so I could get some help, but I felt that I could wait a little longer and I asked her to pray with me. I was sure God would answer us because everything had gone right so far. He would take care of this as well. We began to pray, and didn't stop until I fell asleep. When I woke up the pain was gone and didn't come back for the rest of our vacation.

Mary and I had planned almost every hour of the week. We had many sightseeing trips that kept us busy, but we were always on the lookout for the President or anyone else we might recognize. While walking along Pennsylvania Avenue in front of the White House, we heard someone speak to us. "Where are you going?"

It was late evening, and at first we couldn't see where the voice had come from. All of a sudden, a man burst from the guardhouse with a broom in his hands and chased a big rat across the lawn. It was such a comical sight that we had to stop and watch. Having been outrun by the rodent, the guard turned and came back over to where we stood. Again he asked, "Where do you think you're going at this time of night?"

"We're just going for a walk to do some sightseeing", Mary answered.

"It's not safe for you to go any further. You should go back the way you came, but if you want to see the President, walk slowly to the other driveway entrance. If you time it right, you'll see him coming back to the White House."

We thanked him and went on our way. Nearing the corner, we could hear the sounds of motorcycles and the shrill cry of a siren coming our way. We stopped at the corner, and the motorcade made a left turn and drove right past us. As it did, we could see President Dwight D. Eisenhower waving to us from his limousine. Before we started back, another voice called to us from the guardhouse. He told us that no young woman should be walking the streets of Washington D.C. We conversed with him for a while, and he offered to show us the city with his friend who happened to be the first guard we talked to. We figured that since they were White House guards they would be trustworthy, so we agreed to go out with them the next evening.

As we were getting ready the following day, there was a knock on the door of our hotel room. I was in the shower, and Mary was still getting dressed. Neither of us had stayed in a hotel without our parents before, so we were apprehensive. The door was secured by the deadbolt and the chain lock, but Mary was still nervous and asked me what she should do. Poking my head out from the bathroom door, I told her to ask who it was.

"Telegram, ma'am."

I worried that there might be something wrong at home. "Ask them to pass it to you through the door, but leave the chain lock on." I said to Mary.

She opened the door slightly, peeked into the hallway, then screamed and began to laugh. I threw on a robe and came out to see what the commotion was, and there stood Richard and Joyce, our dear friends from church. When we mentioned our trip, they had told us to behave ourselves because they'd be checking in on us. We knew that they would be visiting friends in Virginia, but we never expected them to actually come to Washington. Seeing that we were getting ready to go out, they asked us about our plans for the evening. Neither one of us wanted to tell them that we were going out with a couple of strangers, but we were honest. After we explained how we met the men, Joyce asked us if they were Christians. Our conversations with the guards hadn't gotten nearly that far, but we assumed that they were not.

Their somewhat disappointed reply was "Girls, you know better."

We reminded them that the men were guards at the White House, and it did make them feel a bit better. "We just wanted to see the area, and thought that would be a safe way to do it." I said.

"Well, let us pray with you and we'll get going", said Richard.

Before they left, Mary and I wanted to give them souvenirs, so we ran into the bathroom and raided the medicine cabinet. We asked our friends to close their eyes and hold out their hands. Once they had, we presented them with a disposable razor, shampoo, a bar of soap, and a small box of Ex-Lax. We had a few laughs over our "gifts", gave hugs and kisses, and said goodbye. Once the door closed, Mary and I began to regret our decision to go out with the guards. We didn't have any way of reaching them, so we decided to take a chance. They turned out to be perfect gentlemen, and we had a great time. When the evening came to an end, I thanked the Lord for watching over us.

Once our vacation was over and I was back to work, I began having pain in my side again. One morning, it was so bad that I stayed home from work. My parents called the doctor's office, and were told to get me to the emergency room right away. I hoped that it was my appendix, so that it could be taken care of quickly. I couldn't afford to take unpaid time off from work.

The doctors determined that I did have appendicitis, but that wasn't all. During surgery, they also found that I had adhesions on my bowel that were caused by the colitis I had battled for so many years. Instead of a small incision on my right side, I ended up with a large cut up the front of my stomach. I was only supposed to be in the hospital for a week, but when the surgeon tried to remove my stitches, the incision began to re-open. It was another seven days before I had healed enough to go home, and another six weeks before my doctor gave me permission to return to work. I had to keep calling my boss to update him on my condition, and reassure him that I would be returning to my job. The upside to my slow recovery was that my dad temporarily kept his hands off me.

When I returned to work, I had to recover from the interruption of a steady income. Getting a few raises (which brought my income to two hundred and eighty dollars a month) helped get me closer to my goal of moving out. I wanted more in my life than just working and coming home to the same old game of hide and seek between my dad and me. When winter came, there was not much to do but stay indoors. I often visited David and his wife just so I would be out of my father's reach. Many nights, I still cried myself to sleep. At least I had my own bedroom. I loved being able to shut the door, sit at my desk, and write a letter to my friend at college, or read my Bible and pray. It was comforting, but not what I longed for. I wanted a husband and a family to love. "When, Lord?!"

It seemed that some of the men I worked with were no better than my dad. I assumed that in an office environment I would be working with people who had more class than the kids I went to school with. It wasn't the case. They were the same crude, obnoxious jerks - just a bit older and disguised in a suit and tie. One of the men made lewd remarks to me in the office, and even drove alongside of me as I walked home from work, trying to get me into his car. Another seemingly nice co-worker had offered me a ride home from work. It seemed much safer than waiting for the bus in a bad neighborhood until I found out that he was married. It was one of the other girls in the office that clued me in. She told me that I'd get myself into trouble if I kept accepting rides from him, because our other co-workers disapproved. I later realized that she was the only one who disapproved, as the two of them were having an affair. Getting a ride from a married man was better than standing out in the cold or rainy weather, though, even if it was a bit tricky at times. Sometimes my dad would walk to my last bus stop so I wouldn't have to walk home in the dark. If he had caught me in the car with my co-worker, I would have been in big trouble. I always had the man drop me off a couple of blocks from the bus stop, usually telling him I had an errand to run on my way home. I didn't understand why my dad felt it was necessary to walk me home. He didn't do it after choir practice or when I came home from a youth activity.

Fortunately, the usual routine of going to work then trying to avoid my dad was interrupted when my mom told me that Edna would be coming for a visit. I was overjoyed because I loved Edna and because it meant that my dad would leave me alone for a week. He would have to put his Christian face on. Fervent prayer and recitation of Bible verses were the core of his act. It was always interesting to hear the points that Aunt Edna would occasionally raise in disagreement with my father's points of view.

Life was good while she stayed at our house. Instead of having to make my own dinner, my parents waited to eat until I came home. Conversation at the table was always interesting. I loved to hear about my cousins' lives, and everything that was going on in their town.

That Friday evening, all of my friends from church were going tobogganing. Without a car, I was unable to go along. As I ate dinner, the phone rang. Mom got up from her chair and answered. I could hear the conversation and my heart jumped for joy. It was Joyce, our choir director's wife. Mom called me over to the phone and said that Joyce wanted to speak with me. I was happy to hear her offer to drive me to the toboggan run. However, I had a feeling my mother would not allow it and I was right. She was still concerned that I had not sufficiently healed from my surgery. I relayed her answer to Joyce, and she immediately dismissed my mother's apprehension.

"Janeen, that's silly. Your mother is wrong. She should let you go! You get dressed and we'll come pick you up. You have half an hour to convince her."

Richard and Joyce both knew very few details of my home life, but I had let them know that he had a violent temper. They were also aware of how controlling he was. At twenty years old I was still rarely allowed to go on a date, and even group activities were subject to scrutiny.

After hanging up the phone and walking back into the kitchen to finish my dinner, Edna caught on that something was wrong. Once more my mother voiced her opposition. I got up from the table to wash my dishes and my heart was heavy with loneliness. I felt like a prisoner in a house of horrors. Finishing the dishes, I walked through the house to my bedroom, closed the door, and let the tears flow down my face.

Soon there was a knock at my door with a quiet, unfamiliar cadence. I opened the door, and there stood Aunt Edna. "May I come in?" she asked.

Still crying, I said "sure" sat back down on the bed.

"Janeen, you know I was a nurse for many years. Now I know how you want to go on that outing, and you should. You get yourself ready and I will handle things here. Can you call your friend back and see if they can pick you up?"

"No, they are already on their way here. They said to keep trying." I explained.

"Well then it's set. You get ready and leave the rest to me."

Feeling reassured that it was the right thing to do, I scrambled to get ready. Anxiety over whether or not my parents would still forbid me from going nearly made me sick. Then there was another knock at my door. This time it was my mom, who told me that Edna had convinced her it would be alright for me to go tobogganing. My dad wanted me home early, but that wasn't going to happen. We were all going out for something to eat after we were done at the park. Edna would surely stick up for me, so I wasn't going to be in any hurry to get home.

Once we were on our way, the questions began. "How old are you now? Why do your parents always make it so difficult for you to go out? How have you been getting to choir practice?"

When Richard and Joyce learned that I was taking two busses each way and in all kinds of weather while my dad slept, they were outraged. That was also the first time they had seen my neighborhood, and it made them very concerned for my safety. They offered to take me to choir practice or any of the youth activities. It was one of the most helpful and appreciated things anyone has ever done for me. Before dropping me off at home that evening, they reminded me, "We will be praying for you. Don't ever think you're imposing on us. We're happy to do this."

Their gesture didn't sit well with mom and dad, though. It made dad look bad, so he made excuses and diverted the conversation. "It's fifteen miles to the church! Do you know how much I would have to spend on gas? And why are you complaining to people about me? After all we have done for you kids and now you talk about me behind my back? Just who do you think you are anyway?!"

I thought he would feel obligated to get me to church after that, but it didn't have quite that strong of an impact. The following week I took the bus to choir practice again. Richard asked me how I got there, which put me in a tough spot. I didn't want to lie, but I also didn't want to tell them that my dad still would not give me a ride. He would definitely find out what I had said and would get angry again. Then I thought, "What difference does it make anyway? I have to deal with him no matter what, so why not tell the truth and see what happens?"

Richard frowned and shook his head in annoyance. "We'll be taking you home tonight."

I thanked him, but was really worried. Dad would interpret Richard and Joyce's help as meddling, and would blame me for involving them. Practice ended, and while we were all talking the thought occurred to me that my dad might have decided to come to the church to pick me up. Excusing myself, I made my way to the parking lot to look for him. If he had come all that way just to find that I had gotten a ride from someone else, there would be a hefty price to pay. I stepped outside, glanced around, and sure enough – he was sitting in the car waiting for me. "Thank you, Lord, for putting that thought in my head." I prayed.

I signaled to my father that I'd be right back, and then went inside the church to tell Richard that I wouldn't need a ride. His offer stood, however. "I would like you to tell your father that from now on we will pick you up and take you home for all activities. You let him know, will you?"

"Yes", I said, "But I'm not sure how he'll respond to that."

"I'll talk with him on Sunday about it", said Richard.

Sunday came, and as he had promised Richard pulled my dad aside and spoke with him. It was settled – from then on I rode with them to every social activity as well as every choir practice. Richard and Joyce were a very big influence for me, and I am still very thankful that God put them in my life.

Chapter 13

Deadline

Even though my social life had improved, my home life had not. My dad constantly wanted to remind us who was in control, and my fight to spend time with friends continued. While I was getting ready for church, he'd often start badgering me. "Where do you think you're going?"

"I'm going to church", I explained as if he didn't already know. "I thought it was ok."

"Well it isn't, so there!" He'd bark.

"What are you saying? I can't go?"

"You will go when I say you can, and not one minute before! Do you understand me?!"

The only answer I dared to give was "yes".

"Then sit down until I tell you that you can leave!" It was the same routine over and over, only to let me go anyway. He just enjoyed watching us squirm.

Anything could set Dad off. If the weather was too hot for his liking, if there were too many bills, or if his hay fever was bothering him the rest of us knew that we would have to tread lightly in his presence. Many times I couldn't even find safety in my own room. A closed door only served as an invitation for him to sneak up very quietly and then fling it open, rushing in to see if I was in the middle of changing my clothes. Sitting at my desk writing a letter to my friend, I would suddenly find my sweater being pulled up over my head. With my arms pulled up over my head, I had to fight to keep my sweater on and try not to fall from my chair onto the hardwood floor.

That was it. Between my father and the men at work I felt dirty and thought no one could ever love me the way they should. I wanted the love that God had planned for a man and a woman; tender, compassionate, forgiving, and respectful. One night in April of 1958, I cried out to the Lord for his help in finding a husband within the next six months, and then I waited.

Those six months were as tortuous as any others, but I was getting my teeth fixed, buying some new clothes, and saving some money when I could. Autumn came, and there will still no young men on my radar. In October, my deadline was only one week away. I said a prayer to remind God of my request, but believed that it would go unanswered. After all this time, why would someone come along now?

At the "college and career" group service on the following Friday night, I sat next to my good friend Mary. She touched my arm and motioned for me to look at the row behind us. When I turned and glanced back, I saw a dark haired, dark eyed young man, and my heart leaped inside me. He was so good looking! I made up my mind that I would try to speak with him after church. After all, hadn't we just heard a sermon on reaching out to people and welcoming them when they come to our services?

Normally it would have been very difficult for me to approach a visitor to welcome them and invite them back. I was very backward and had no self confidence. That night, however, God had made me feel self-assured. When the service ended, I had a plan of action ready. I would start out for the ladies room, which would give me the chance to look around the lobby and see if he might be standing around. If not, I could go into the ladies room for a minute and give him a chance to come out into the lobby. Walking out of the sanctuary, I surveyed the lobby and didn't see him. Rounding the corner to head toward the restroom, I saw him just as he stopped to get a drink of water at the fountain. As he straightened up I introduced myself, and he told me his name.

All in one breath I said, "We're glad to have you visit our church, and we'd love to have you back on Sunday morning."

As he looked at me, I was sure that this could be the man for me. But the next words out of his mouth were disappointing. "I have my own church that I attend on Sunday morning."

With little left to say I once again thanked him for coming. He left and I moved on, waiting for my ride home. In the car Joyce asked me whom I'd been speaking with. I told her as much as I knew, which wasn't much.

All weekend I thought of him, wondering if he would come back to our church. Sunday morning arrived, and I was just as eager to see him. "Would he, or wouldn't he?" I thought. Filing onto the platform with the rest of the choir, I scanned the worshippers to see if I could spot him, but no…he wasn't there.

That afternoon I went home, ate dinner, washed the dishes, and went to my room for a nap. Once I lay down I began to weep. "Lord, what happened?! I was so sure that you were letting me know this was the man. How could I be so wrong? I want to get away from my dad, but I have no money. I want to get married, and it seems to be the only way out! Lord, please!"

I felt that God had really let me down. This was the end of the six months, and the one man I saw as a potential answer to prayer would probably never cross my path again. I sobbed until I fell asleep, a wonderful escape from my disappointment and frustration.

An hour or two later I woke up to get ready for choir practice without thinking of him at all. Sunday evening was again time for me to join the rest of the choir on the platform. Joyce was standing in the same row as me, with two people between us. She held the hymnal all the way up in front of her face, which must have looked strange to the congregation. She was looking at me, trying to get my attention.

"Psst! Psst!" she tried unsuccessfully to be discrete.

Looking down the row at her, I saw her finger pointing forward into the hymnal. The first thing I saw when I looked out was her husband who was signaling us to stop the nonsense. Then I saw what she was really trying to show me. There he stood, singing along with the rest of the congregation. It was the handsome visitor I had met on Friday evening. He knew all the words to the hymns…he must be a Christian! My head was swimming with questions. Would someone else get him? How could I get to him first? If the did, then I would have to accept that he was not the one God had chosen for me. I decided not to change my normal routine. After the service I always went to the front of the sanctuary to pray. He would either go down as well or he would wait for me. But if he should happen to ask me out, what would I do?

The choired filed down from the platform, and the only place left for my friend Mary and I to sit was at the back of the sanctuary. Mary had also noticed that he was back. "Did you see who's here? Are you going to talk to him?" she asked.

"Yes, if he's still here after prayer time."

Later, when I had finished praying, I began walking up the aisle. There he was, sitting at the end of a row. I would have to walk past him. Was that his plan all along? Had he come back for me? Where was my dad? Was he watching me? I could see my mom standing at the back of the church talking with a friend.

His dark eyes looking up at me took my breath away. His hair was almost black with a little gray at the temples, and he wore a dark blue suit. Needless to say, I thought he looked great. As I came near him I could see he wanted to say something to me, so I stopped to say "hello".

After I asked how he was, he began to drive the conversation. I sat down in the pew behind him to avoid blocking the aisle. We continued to chat, and then he asked me out for coffee. I tried to restrain my excitement as I accepted his offer.

"You can have more than a cup of coffee", he added.

He had no idea how happy I'd be with just a coffee as long as it meant I could be with him. My dad would surely be an obstacle, though. "Lord", I prayed, "if this is your plan you're going to have to create another miracle. How will I ever be able to get my dad to let me go out with someone he's never seen before?"

Once again the Lord had it all planned out for me. Excusing myself, I hurried into the ladies room to make sure I looked just right. All the other girls were there, chattering away about the new guy. Joyce came looking for me a few seconds later.

"How did it go?!" she asked.

"Great" I exclaimed, and then realized I had a minor problem "but I don't remember his name!"

Joyce was ready to help any way she could. "Don't worry, I will find out for you. Just give me a minute."

By this time we had the attention of all the other girls. I told them about my date, and the look of disbelief on their faces said it all.

One of them actually said, "You?! How did *that* happen?!" She was obviously jealous, and all of them were aware that my father hardly ever let me date.

Joyce came back to tell me that his name was Gil, and that she found out that he attended her mother's church.

"But now I have to deal with my parents." I reminded her. "You know they're not going to let me go out with him. I'm just going to have to do what I want to this time."

She thought about it for a second, and then said "I'll have a talk with your mom. You just go."

Joyce kept her word. She left me and immediately went to my mother and told her my story. Joyce explained that her mother (who was visiting our church that evening) knew Gil, and that he faithfully attended church. My mother said with apprehension, "Joyce, I am not the problem. It's Stephen. He just doesn't want her dating, and he doesn't know the young man at all. But…" she paused, "I'll take your word for it."

I caught up with the two of them, and told my mom in my own words about Gil and the date. She was still worried and said she didn't know what she'd tell my father, but Joyce intervened again. "Don't worry, Verna! I will handle him. Where is he?"

"He's in a deacon's meeting, and I don't know when he will be out."

I will always believe that God had his hand in the situation, and gave Joyce the right words when she spoke with my dad. When he came out of the meeting, she gently chastised him about the restrictions he was still imposing on me even though I was twenty years old. He finally caved in and said, "Alright, if you feel he is ok, then I will trust your judgment."

That evening was the first in a week of wonderful dates. I barely even saw my dad until the weekend. With each passing day I grew more and more convinced that God had sent Gil to me. He was so caring and such a gentleman that I was having a hard time believing it was going to last. I was sure that once he found out about my past he would no longer be interested in me.

Saturday morning was usually a relaxed time when Mom would make a big breakfast for us, and we would go our separate ways after eating. This particular Saturday was a bit different. As I cleared the table, Dad started with the questions. "So tell me about this guy you have been going out with. Is he a Christian? Does he smoke? Does he drink? Are his parents Christians? Where does he go to church?" I didn't even have a chance to answer one question before he blurted out the next one.

Finally I had a chance to catch up and responded to his inquisition. Then came another question. "You said he went to college. Which college, and what did he study?"

"Well, he went to Michigan State University and is a graduate of the School of Psychology." My father's dismay was communicated clearly with his expression.

"Well he had better not come around here psychoanalyzing anyone!" He eased his tone a little and said "You need to invite him over so I can meet this guy."

"Ok, Lord..." I thought. "I'm trusting you to take care of all of this."

On our date that evening, I knew I must slowly start letting Gil know about my family. "God, help me to say the right things. I have no idea how to go about this. I love him and I am so afraid I will scare him away. Please let him be the one, and give him an understanding and compassionate heart."

First I told Gil that he had been invited to dinner. It made him happy, but he could see that I was not. "What's the problem? Don't you want me to meet your folks?"

"Not really", I said. "Oh, Mom is fine and I think you will like her, but it's my dad." There. I said it.

"Why? What's wrong with your dad?"

I told him as little as possible, only saying that my father was very domineering and leaving the rest for later. I could only hope that Dad wouldn't give him a hard time. We made plans for Gil to come over the next day after church.

Gil and I went to church together, then back to my house. Dinner was nice enough, but it wasn't long before my father started in with his questions. "Are you a Christian? Where do you go to church? How do you know you're a Christian? Do you smoke?"

My dad was so rude that I was sure Gil would never ask me out again. When it was time for the evening service, Gil and I left the house and got into his car. I was sure he was about to tell me that he would not be seeing me anymore. It was quite the opposite. We talked about my father's expectations for my future. They were not very high. I could marry the garbage man, just as long as he was a Christian.

Gil could see through my dad's feigned indifference toward the occupation of my future husband. "Well I can see why he would say that. It's because he's a janitor, and he he'd still be one step above a garbage man in his own mind."

Hearing Gil's comment made me hopeful that he would accept me in spite of my home life. After the evening service, we went to a restaurant where Gil began to ask me some questions about my family. It was a long evening. I filled him in on some of the details, but left out others. I just couldn't bear to lose him so soon.

Later that week it was my turn to meet his parents. It was scary for me because I had never dated someone long enough to be introduced to his family. What would I wear? What would I say? And most importantly…what if they don't like me?

After work on Thursday, Gil came by the house to pick me up. We went out for pizza, and he told me about his family. Since he was an only child, I only had two people to meet. We finished our dinner and went to his house. Meeting his father was easy; he was a short man with a brush cut of thick white hair. He made me feel at ease, and conversation came naturally. Gil's mother was at church, so I had some time to get to know his father.

As we talked, I saw headlights turning into the driveway. My heart began to beat a little faster, because mothers don't always approve of the girl their son picks out. I remained sitting on the living room couch as Gil's mother came in through the front door. She raised her arms to remove her hat as she looked my way. I got the impression that she wasn't very happy to see me. Without saying a word she moved forward to the coat closet where she placed her hat on the shelf and removed her coat. The three of us still sat, waiting for her to join us. Instead, she walked past the living room and into the kitchen. Gil was annoyed. He got up and went after her to find out what was the matter. He brought her back to the living room, and she was visibly unhappy. Gil introduced us, and after we shook hands, she returned to the kitchen. She was the opposite of her husband, but we didn't let her spoil our evening.

Leaving his house, Gil and I talked about our families and our future. We stopped at a nearby park, and we continued to talk in the car. Over the course of the three weeks we had been dating, I had told him all there was to know about my father and the abuse I had grown up with. That night I disclosed the few remaining details that, in fairness to him, I felt he should know. I felt comfortable that he still wanted to be with me, or I wouldn't have been in sitting in his car.

He put his arm around me and pulled me close. He looked into my eyes and said, "I know we haven't been dating very long, but I want to marry you if you will have me. You don't have to answer me right away, but I know what I want and I think you do too."

My heart was pounding so hard I could almost hear it. "I don't have to wait to give you the answer…I already know just what I want. I will marry you if you will have me after everything I've told you about my past."

That was the most wonderful evening of my life. I knew for sure that God had placed this man in my life to love and care for me with the understanding I needed.

We had set a date of May 9, which gave us 8 months to plan our wedding. It didn't seem like much time, but I knew it would work out because as the Bible says, "If God is for us, who can be against us?"

I still didn't have a lot of money saved, so I wasn't sure how I'd be able to afford a wedding dress, let alone a vale. The other thing I had to think about was choosing my bridesmaids. It was easy to pick my maid of honor. Joyce had been so helpful to me during the last year that I had to ask her. I was worried that she may not be able to do it since she had already been in so many weddings that year, but I wanted to at least ask her. To my surprise and delight, she happily agreed to be my maid of honor.

After the Sunday morning service a few weeks later, Joyce pulled me aside to talk privately. She said cautiously, "I've had something on my mind, and I don't know how you'll take this. I don't want to hurt your feelings..." I thought for sure she was going to back out of the wedding. "Have you picked out a dress yet?" I was relieved by her question.

"No, not yet", I replied.

"I'd be happy to offer you my gown if you don't mind wearing a used wedding dress. We wear the same size, so I think it will fit you nicely. You and Gil can come over for dessert sometime this week and then you can try it on."

My mind flashed back to her wedding and the beautiful dress she wore. Her father owned a small business and earned enough money to pay for a wonderful wedding. I gladly accepted her offer. This couple had been so good to me, and once again helping me beyond my dreams.

Gil picked me up on Tuesday after work, and we drove to Joyce's house. We were really hoping the dress would fit me. If it didn't, I was just going to have to find an inexpensive formal dress instead of a proper wedding gown. That wouldn't have been the way I had dreamed of my wedding day, but the important thing was that I would be married.

After visiting for a while, Joyce and I went into her bedroom so I could try on the dress. From the time she mentioned it to me, I prayed it would fit and that I would like the way it looked on me. First I put on the stiff slip that would hold out the skirt a bit. Then came the dress. I could hardly bear the anticipation. I didn't care that it was a hand-me-down. I was used to wearing secondhand clothing, and was just glad to have it.

Once my arms were in the sleeves and the top button was fastened, I was sure it was going to fit. I continued closing up the back of the gown and with each button I turned, my heart swelled until I could hold back no longer and began to cry with joy. I looked in the mirror, and neither of us could believe how well the dress fit. The only thing it needed was to be cleaned.

I still had to get a vale, shoes, hand bag, and gifts for the girls. I was running out of money, and had to make ends meet without my parents' help. My dad was very unhappy that I was getting married. He had to get in his last few kicks during my final days around the house. He would often hide in my bedroom or behind a door, then jump out and scare me. Some Friday nights he would stay up with all the lights off just so he could pull that trick when Gil dropped me off. If I came home five minutes past my eleven o'clock curfew, he would grab me and give me a piece of his mind. One of his favorite threats was "Why, I ought to clean your clock!" Then he'd add, "I'll be glad when you're out of here. Good riddance!"

I went to bed each night asking God not to let anything hinder us from getting married. I still had a hard time believing my prayers were really being answered. Had I actually found a good Christian man who would really love me and even pray for me? Praises were always on my mind. I couldn't stop thinking about how much I loved Gil.

The Sunday before our wedding, I was just about ready for Gil to come over when I heard my mom call for me. I left the bathroom and went into the kitchen to find my mom walking toward me, upset over something. "Janeen, can you help me with my hair? It keeps sticking up over here and here" she said as she pointed to her unruly locks.

I sized up the situation, and figured out what needed to be done. I lightly brushed through her hair with my fingers, explaining what I would do. As I did, my father came stomping into the dining room and shouted, "What are you doing, yelling at your mother that way?!"

"Stephen, it's ok! She is just trying to help me with her hair" my mother replied, puzzled by his anger.

Pushing past my mom, he yelled "I'll show her", and tried to grab me.

"Stephen! What are you doing?! I said she was only trying to help me with my hair because I was having trouble with it!" She might just as well have been talking to a brick wall.

"I don't care! She's not getting away with it!"

I ran around the kitchen table so he couldn't get me, but he kept coming. I fled past Mom and into the dining room with Dad still hot on my tail. I circled to the back of the dining table, and my dad stood on the opposite side yelling at me. "You think you are something, marrying that big college boy! I'll show you a thing or two!

He spotted a metal petit four serving dish, and picked it up with his finger through the ring handle at the top. He brought it up, ready to swing it at my head saying "I'll show you! Just who do you think you are?!"

I was saved by the bell. Gil had arrived at the front door to pick me up for church. He was able to calm me down on the way, and that was the last physical confrontation I had with my dad.

The next Friday, my co-workers threw a surprise shower for me. They all chipped in and gave me a set of pots and pans, and a few other kitchen utensils. It was a very nice gesture that I never expected. Our rehearsal was later that evening. My parents refused to help because my father was resentful about losing his control over me, and he was jealous of Gil's parents. He had told me "If you're going to get married, it'll be up to you to pay. I don't have any money and even if I did, I wouldn't give it to you. You don't need to make such a big splash about getting married! You like his family so much, let them pay! You are over there all the time!"

I wasn't even allowed to have Gil in our house at night, so we either went to his house or sat and talked in his car.

Gil's mother and father took it upon themselves to host dinner at their house. When we arrived, I felt very sad and frustrated over the situation. This was something my parents ought to be doing, and everyone present knew it. I just reminded my self that it would all be over tomorrow. "Just be yourself and be happy" I thought.

The dinner was wonderful, and everyone had a nice time except for our parents.

I was awake by seven a.m. the next morning. The wedding wasn't until much later in the afternoon, but I was much to excited to go back to sleep so I decided to double check the things I had packed for the honeymoon. Finding everything in its place, I waited in my room until I heard the rest of the family up and about. I heard Mom first, then Dad, and then I smelled the aroma of coffee brewing.

I stepped out into the dining room, and caught a whiff of fresh air drifting through the window. It was a beautiful May morning, with the sun shining brightly and a warm breeze blowing gently. I went outside to meet the mailman, who delivered cards from friends unable to attend the wedding. Dad was strangely quiet until we were almost done with breakfast. He said that he wished us the best, and hoped I would be happy. "I guess you want to get going to the apartment to get ready, so get your things together and we will go." They were the very words I wanted to hear.

Mom helped grandpa get ready, and Dad loaded up the car. On the way to my future home we were all silent, each one lost in their own thoughts. Rick was sad that I was leaving, my mom regretted her inability to stop my father, my grandfather was losing his caretaker, and my dad faced the revelation of his true nature.

A flood of thoughts and emotion rushed through my mind as I walked down the aisle. The foremost was the excitement for a new beginning. When I saw Gil standing at the front of the sanctuary, I was filled with so much joy that I wanted to shout out my praise to the Lord in Heaven for this moment. Then there was the man walking me down the aisle. What must be going through his mind right now? I could only imagine. I wanted to tell everyone there what he really was. A terrible, wicked father, awful husband, and shameful son; anything but a Christian. But I knew it would only spoil my wedding. I just looked ahead to my new life and knew it would be much better.

I wanted to laugh and cry at the same time. God had answered my prayers in a way that could not be ignored or dismissed as coincidence. The man I had specifically described to Him in my prayers for a husband was standing just a few feet away waiting to marry me. God's plan for this season of my life had come to fruition, and I was truly overshadowed by His love.

Chapter 14

A New Life

As the years passed and Gil and I were raising our family, we rarely visited my parents. Birthdays and holidays were about the only time we went to their home, and it was only for my mom's sake that we went at all. Neither of us thought it would be wise for them to spend much time around my father. If Gil was home, they were both welcome to visit, but if he was not, only my mother was allowed in our house.

My brother David had allowed the cycle of violence to continue in his own family. He had become the very person he had hated so much. In poor health and facing a failing marriage, he ended his life at the age of twenty eight. He left behind three small children, two of whom were living with Gil and me because of the turmoil in their home. I was also pregnant with our third child.

I was grateful that my father was in the hospital at the time. None of us knew how he might have reacted to the news had he not been so ill. My mother visited him later that evening with Gil and me. We walked into his room and found him sitting on the edge of his bed, rocking back and forth saying, "This is all my fault. This is all my fault, isn't it?"

None of us denied it. He asked us for the details, and we recounted the day's grim events. Again he assumed the blame for David's suicide, yet he never said he was sorry.

Five years after David's death we moved to a small town outside of Syracuse, New York. Gil and I grew in the Lord and raised our children in a safe, loving environment. We became a very close-knit family. A couple of years later, my mother passed away, and my father turned to us for help and support. Regardless of all the things he had done, Gil and I never refused to help him when the need arose. God had allowed me to truly forgive my dad, and it gave me the freedom to show him love in spite of the past.

One day, he called to ask if he could come for a visit. Gil thought that he would be in too much grief to cause trouble. He was also in poor health, and in our home he would be unlikely to try anything so we agreed to let him stay with us. Aside from several attempts to impart Biblical wisdom to us (which I found nearly impossible to tolerate) things did go well. He stayed with us for a few days, then went back home to Michigan.

Shortly after that we moved to Baltimore, Maryland. Dad began calling on a regular basis just to talk. He was very lonely and had too much time on his hands and too many thoughts running through his mind.

One afternoon he called to say he had started dating Rose. She was a friend of my mother and had been my Sunday school and Junior Church teacher when I was a child. Her parents and mine had been friends for years. Her husband had passed away several years before mom's death.

Once again he called, and had a question that shocked me. "Do you think it would be OK for me to marry Rose?" he asked.

My first concern was for Rose. "Dad...please doesn't treat her like you did mom."

"Oh, no I won't! I promise."

They were married just nine months after my mother passed away, and eventually moved to Florida.

On their only visit back to Michigan, I was eight months pregnant with our fourth child, Chris. We were not invited to visit then in Florida so we never went. The phone calls were very few and far between. They were busy taking care of Rose's parents, and had done some traveling. One day Rose called to let us know that dad had a stroke and was in the hospital. Gil and I were unable to go but Rick made the trip to help them. After Dad's brush with death he began wanting to see us. He called Rick and me regularly to invite us to visit, but I was not ready to spend the money or the time to see him. Our oldest son had started college, and we didn't have much expendable income. I had no idea how much Rose knew about our family history, and this complicated the situation even more.

In 1984, Gil had started a new job that offered him the benefit of a company car. It was a great blessing, since our car was having some engine trouble and the air conditioning was no longer working. On a cold day in February, we took the car in to have it fixed. It was going to be mine after the repairs were finished. After finding out the cost, Gil said he had something he wanted to talk about. As I listened to him speak, I couldn't believe my ears!

"I think it's time for you to go to Florida to visit your dad and Rose", he said. "Things went well for Rick and his family when they went to Florida, and they've even gone back a few times."

I still thought he might be kidding and I couldn't help but question him about why he had come to this decision.

He explained, "I think the stroke may have caused him to realize his own mortality. He may want a chance to talk with you and ask for forgiveness. I don't know if it will happen, but I think he should have the chance. I want you to take Pam and Chris with you. He won't try anything with you there."

He did have a point, and I missed Rose. Every time I talked to her on the phone, she was her same sweet self that I had remembered from my childhood. Upon reflecting on those things I began to feel that God was telling me that the time was right.

Then I began to ask myself: How am I going to do this? I had never taken any road trips without Gil, let alone driven across five states. However, I felt this trip was the Lord's will and I was up to the challenge. Once Pam had agreed to it we then told Chris he was going on a long trip to visit his grandpa who he had never seen. He was seven years old and was excited to be skipping school and going to Disney World.

We then made a call was to let Rose and Dad know that we would finally accept their invitation. They were overjoyed, and wanted to know right away how soon we could come and how long we would stay.

It was an unusually warm day for being the middle of February when Pam, Chris, and I said goodbye to Gil and were off to Florida. Just before reaching Ohio and less than one hour from home, Pam and I heard Chris's voice from the back seat. "How much longer will it be?" I hadn't expected to hear that question quite so soon.

It had been raining from the time we started out and I was so hoping for better weather but we weren't so lucky. Once we reached Ohio the car jerked fiercely even though that was supposed to be fixed. Pam and I looked at each other for a moment wondering if we should turn back, but we decided to continue on unless it got worse. The rain turned to ice and snow, and conflicts between independent truckers and Teamsters who were on strike brought even more uncertainty. I just kept reminding myself how sure Gil and I had felt about this being the right time for me to go and see Dad.

A day later we crossed from Georgia into Florida and were happy to be out of the bad weather. After a few more miles we stopped for gas. I pulled up to the pump, got out of the car, then poked my head back inside and said, "Oh my, you have got to get out of the car and stretch your legs. You won't believe how warm it is!"

We heard tree frogs for the first time and saw our first palm trees and orange groves. What a place to be when we had experienced such brutal weather just the day before. It was hard to believe we were really in Florida.

When we arrived at my parents' house we were greeted by Rose with open arms and kisses. Dad waited inside for us. He looked astonishingly different compared to the last time I saw him. He had very little hair, eyes that could no longer see and hands and feet that were numb from diabetes. He had lost a lot of weight. After a few minutes of greetings and conversation, dad asked Rose if she could get him over to the couch. We watched as she told us what she had to do to help him be mobile. Very gently and carefully she pulled him up from the chair he was sitting in, and once he was steady she then turned around with her back facing him and had him put his hands on her shoulders. As she began to walk, she dictated each step.

"Right foot...left foot...right foot...left foot", she said as they walked in sync to the couch.

"Ok, now turn around and go ahead and sit down." They faced each other for a moment until he eased himself onto the cushion of the sofa.

Rose excused herself, saying she needed to finish fixing dinner and would give us some time alone to talk.

Dad spoke first and it scared me. It wasn't because he spoke first, but because of words he spoke and the familiar gesture that accompanied them. "Sis, come sit next to me" he said as he reached out his arm and curled his index finger a couple of times to beckon me toward him. Pam was aware of some of the things he had done, and we exchanged a wary glance.

I quickly prayed and asked God for wisdom and I knew Gil was praying about the whole situation. In spite of my fear, I decided to walk over and sit next to him. I was not prepared for what happened next. Dad leaned toward me and whispered. "Sis will you forgive me?"

I wanted to be sure there was no misunderstanding. "For what, dad?"

"You know…all those awful things I did to you at home."

I was blown away. I hadn't been in the house for fifteen minutes and he was saying the words I thought I would never hear.

"Dad, I forgave you a long time ago when I was still a teenager."

He started to cry and asked "How could you forgive me?"

"I had to forgive you if I wanted my prayers answered."

He had memorized many verses of the Bible, and knew what it said about forgiveness. Rose wondered why it was so quiet asked if everything was ok. Dad spoke up, "Yes, it is now".

The days we spent at their home were very interesting. When my dad found out that our car wasn't running well, he asked Rose to take us to the repair shop where their car had been fixed. They even loaned me their car so I could take the kids to the beach and to an alligator show. It was quite a change from times past when Dad said "If you come down for a visit, you had better drive or rent a car, because you're not going to use mine."

It was one of many examples of how much the Lord had worked in his life, and reinforced my belief that all things are possible with God. From then on our relationship was completely different. We visited whenever we could and checked in on them often. My brother and his family also made trips to see our parents, and even helped them repair their home.

Chapter 15

Forgiveness

As my father lay motionless in his hospital bed, Rick and I stood over him listening for a moment to the machines that monitored his vital signs and filled his lungs with oxygen. Rose sat in a chair and watched him intently.

I reflected on how different my life was from my childhood, and how far the Lord had brought me. He had delivered me from such incredible darkness into exactly the life for which I had hoped and prayed. I had been happily married for over thirty years. With God's help I was able to raise four children without perpetuating the sins of my father, and all of them were serving the Lord. The emotional and physical scars of abuse remained, but with God's help I had not allowed them to destroy my future.

Dad was struggling to stay with us just a little longer, and the three of us knew why. Since my first visit to Florida, he had asked Rick and me to forgive him several times. I reminded him each time that I had forgiven him long before he had even asked, but until that night in the hospital my brother had not been able to release him from his guilt. Our dad had missed his opportunity for forgiveness from David, but he was asking one more time for our forgiveness and we had to grant it.

Gently squeezing his hand I said once more, "Dad, it's ok. I forgive you."

Rick spoke as well. "I forgive you too, Dad. You don't have to feel guilty anymore. I forgive you."

Almost as if someone had flipped a switch, our father's heart rate began to slow down. His eyes closed and he drifted off, free from his disease and his guilt.

Epilogue

While the subject matter dealt with in this book is dark and sometimes disturbing, it is not intended to sadden or shock. Instead, I hope it can be a comfort and encouragement for anyone who is trapped in an abusive relationship, or has been deeply hurt in any way by someone they've trusted. I also hope my story can also be an encouragement for strength in the face of overwhelming trials. While writing this book I have prayed and I will continue to pray that it will be a blessing to anyone who reads it.

I believe that the power of forgiveness is clearly demonstrated in my life, and the lives of my brothers and father. As I have pointed out, we are commanded by God to forgive one another, and it is only by His grace that I was able to do so. In turn, I gained a new outlook on my situation and life in general. Furthermore, when my dad finally asked for the forgiveness I had already given him, we enjoyed a restored relationship that would never have been possible with out the life-changing power of Jesus Christ. My brothers and I had eventually broken free from our father's grip, but only two of us had been freed from his influence. My brother David, however, never gave the Lord control of this area of his life. He allowed his hatred and anger to destroy him. Victims of domestic violence often become abusers themselves, but this does not have to be a foregone conclusion. In the same way that a relationship with Jesus Christ can provide you with the strength to forgive, it can also provide you with the strength to break the cycle of violence.

If you have suffered or are suffering through abuse, you are not alone. I hope that sharing my story has given you hope for deliverance. As I grew up in the 1940s and 50s, there were very few places I could turn for help. Today, however, there are many more resources available to victims of domestic violence. If you are a victim, I strongly urge you to contact appropriate authorities such as your local police department or The National Domestic Violence Hotline (1-800-799-3324) for help.

Even though I doubted Him many times, God was truly with me and cared for me even through the direst circumstances. If you are not a believer in Jesus Christ, please consider carefully the gospel, or "good news". This good news begins with the understanding that everyone has sinned and fallen short of the holiness and perfection that God requires.

Mat 5:48	"Therefore you shall be perfect, just as your Father in heaven is perfect."
Rom 3:23	for all have sinned and fall short of the glory of God

Next, the Bible clearly communicates that the consequences of sin are death and judgment.

Rom 6:23   For the wages of sin *is* death, but the gift of God *is* eternal life in Christ Jesus our Lord.

However, hope comes to us through the sacrifice of Jesus Christ who was crucified and died in our place.

Rom 5:8   But God demonstrates His own love toward us, in that while we were still sinners, Christ died for us.

Rom 5:9   Much more then, having now been justified by His blood, we shall be saved from wrath through Him.

We are required to respond to the gospel by acknowledging our sin, turning from it in sincere repentance, and placing our faith in Jesus Christ.

Act 2:38   Then Peter said to them, "Repent, and let every one of you be baptized in the name of Jesus Christ for the remission of sins; and you shall receive the gift of the Holy Spirit.

Eph 2:8   For by grace you have been saved through faith, and that not of yourselves; *it is* the

	gift of God,
Eph 2:9	not of works, lest anyone should boast.

In turn, we can be sure that He will forgive us.

John 3:16	"For God so loved the world that He gave His only begotten Son, that whoever believes in Him should not perish but have everlasting life."

This is, of course, merely an introduction to God's plan of salvation and further guidance should be sought from local church leaders or any Christian friends you may have.

I thank you for reading this book, and once again I hope that it has been a blessing to you.

www.ingramcontent.com/pod-product-compliance
Lightning Source LLC
Chambersburg PA
CBHW031642040426
42453CB00006B/183